Designs for Living and Learning

Designs for Living

and Learning

Transforming Early Childhood Environments

Deb Curtis and Margie Carter

Redleaf Press

© 2003 Deb Curtis and Margie Carter
Photos of Anita Rui Olds by Beth Wallace
Cover and interior design by Percolator

Published by Redleaf Press
            a division of Resources for Child Caring
            450 N. Syndicate, Suite 5
            St. Paul, MN 55104

Visit us online at www.redleafpress.org

Redleaf Press books are available at a special discount when purchased in bulk (1,000 or more copies) for special premiums and sales promotions. For details, contact the sales manager at 800-423-8309.

Library of Congress Cataloging-in-Publication

Curtis, Deb.
  Designs for living and learning : transforming early childhood environments /
Deb Curtis and Margie Carter.
       p. cm.
Includes bibliographical references and index.
  ISBN 1-929610-29-7 (pbk.)
  1. Education, Preschool—United States—Planning. 2. Child care—United States—Planning.
3. Classroom environment—United States. I. Carter, Margie. II. Title.
  LB1140.23.C87 2003
  372.21—dc21
                                        2003002142
Printed in Korea

For Anita Rui Olds
1940–1999

"Children are miracles. Believing that
every child is a miracle can transform the
way we design for children's care. When
we invite a miracle into our lives, we prepare
ourselves and the environment around us.
We may set out flowers or special offerings.
We may cleanse ourselves, the space, or our
thoughts of everything but the love inside us.
We make it our job to create, with reverence
and gratitude, a space that is worthy of a
miracle! Action follows thought. We can
choose to change. We can choose to design
spaces for miracles, not minimums."

—Anita Rui Olds, 1999

Acknowledgments

Child Care Design Lab, Tufts University, Boston, Massachusetts

Many folks around the country have been very generous in allowing us to take photographs of their programs. In recent years, programs familiar and unfamiliar to us have continued to send stories and photos of the exciting transformations they have been making. As we heard about particularly interesting environments and materials, we contacted people to solicit photos. We also pursued stories of directors who successfully negotiated with regulatory bodies so that we could share those as well.

Our special appreciation goes out to the following people who significantly supported our efforts to write this book. At the Burlington Little School, Rhonda Iten and Cindy Hayertz worked with Deb inventing and designing many of the environmental ideas. For five years they have shared the hard work of physically building, organizing, and maintaining a place of living and learning with children and each other—despite the absence of program funds to furnish and supply their preschool classroom. Their classroom and play yard is awesome to visit and is starting to attract national attention.

Over the last ten years Margie has served as the staff trainer for two Seattle programs that are featured prominently throughout this book: Martin Luther King Jr. Day Home Center and Hilltop Children's Center. The lead teachers and director at MLK—Aurora Escano, Deadru Hilliard, and Michael Koetje—have steadily moved their program from a mediocre one to a model one. They have developed meaningful relationships among the children, families, and staff; generated an excitement about learning; and begun a visionary new building now under construction. At Hilltop, the lead teachers—Megan Arnim, Myrna Canon, Sarah Felstiner, and Ann Pelo—have worked to transform themselves and a less than desirable, shared church space into an engaging one, which has been featured in several videos and has gained a national reputation (see appendix A). They have weathered staff and director turnover, personal and program crises, and heartrending loss of life among families in the program—all the while continuing to provide a wonderful place for living and learning. Their new director, Susie Eisman; office manager, Susan Alexander; and staff trainer, Julie Bisson have steadily built an administrative leadership team and organizational structure to keep the program pushing past the continued hardships placed in their way.

Deb and Margie have followed the transformations and built strong collegial relationships of respect with several other programs featured throughout *Designs for Living and Learning*. The Head Start programs at Chicago Commons and the Karen D. Love site of Neighborhood Association House in San Diego have refused to let a bureaucratic mentality or an overwhelming body of regulations and requirements get in their way of creating exceptional programs that value children and families. Each of these programs has transformed how the staff sees their work and the children and their families. Their environments reflect remarkable ingenuity and careful attention to values and relationships. Two family providers— Donna King at Children First, in Durham, North Carolina, and Nancy Gerber in Spokane, Washington—have demonstrated remarkable tenacity and creativity in making joyous places where children are profoundly respected. They have reminded us that family providers are significant members of our profession we can learn from and admire.

Shifting through hundreds of photos that made their way to our home office at Harvest Resources has been a wonderful, but challenging, experience. We extend our apologies to anyone we have unintentionally overlooked or incorrectly identified in the photo captions. We have tried to keep good records, but sometimes the avalanche of examples got away from us. Up to this time our experience with digital photography and managing files with computer technology has been limited, and we are grateful once again to our families and friends who helped us solve problems, brought us flowers and music, fed us, and kept us in good humor. Beth Wallace, Jennifer Shepard, and Jesse Singer at Redleaf Press were tireless in their attention to detail and their commitment to making this a beautiful book.

We weren't able to use all the photographs and stories that were sent to us, but we offer special thanks to those who took the time and effort to get them to us: Cruz Barrios, Jane Cecil, Maria Cruz, Sonia Gonzales, Karen Haigh, Jennifer Keldah, Diane Rodrigous, and Gigi Schroeder at the Chicago Commons Child Development Program, Chicago; Peg Callaghan at Oakton Community College, Des Plaines, Illinois; Barbara Burt, Marcella Prendez, Liz Straub, Mina Sabeghi, and Julie Garrett at Neighborhood House Head Start, San Diego; Angela Ferrario at World Bank Children's Center, managed by Aramark Work Life Partnership, Washington, D.C.; Christie Colunga and Elaine Stockton at Alhambra Head Start, Phoenix; Julie Powers at Dodge Nature School, West Saint Paul, Minnesota; Janis LaDouceur and Don Wong of Barbour/LaDouceur Architects, Minneapolis; Mary Helen Young at the Center for Child and Family Studies, University of California, Davis; Becky Candra at La Jolla Nursery School, La Jolla, California; Vic McMurray at Bridges Family Child Care, Madison, Wisconsin; Lou Host-Jablonski of Design

Coalition, Madison, Wisconsin; Mary Graham at Children's Village, Philadelphia; Laurie Todd, Portland, Oregon; Julie Bullard at University of Montana, Dillon; Stephen Gillette at The Little School, Bellevue, Washington; Donatella Giovannini at Ufficio Educazione degli adulti, Pistoia, Italy; Larry MacMillian, Gina Lewis, and Wanda Biltheimer of Highline Head Start and Puget Sound ESD, Burien, Washington; Penny Gagnon, Sallie Sawin, Jill Carey, and Maryanne Gallagher at University Child Care, University of Massachusetts, Amherst; George Forman at University of Massachusetts, Amherst; Weston Lord, Loc-Kits, Creative Building Systems, North Berwick, Maine; Carmen Masso and Gloria Camacho of La Escuelita Bilingual School, Seattle; Annette Jefferson at We Are the World Day Care, Seattle; Kidspace Child Care Center; Teri Jennings and Pat Shultz of Children's Holladay Center, YMCA, GSA, Portland, Oregon; Alise Shaffer and Lesley Evans, Evergreen Community School, Santa Monica, California; Susanna Federe at Kensington Forest Glen Children's Center, Silver Springs, Maryland; Donna Forman and Judy Haney at Decatur ECEAP, Federal Way, Washington; Steve Franzel, Will Parnell, and Helen Gordon at Child Development Center, Portland, Oregon; Dee Jammal at Smart Start, Dallas; Susan Stacey at Child and Family Development Center at the New Hampshire Technical Institute, Concord, New Hampshire; Jan Gleason and Eileen Tobin of Environmental Works, Seattle; Nancy Gerber's Family Child Care Home, Spokane, Washington; Charlotte Jahn, Marjorie Johnson, Jean Kasota, and Marge A. Sorlie of the Office of Child Care Policy, Seattle; Kathy O'Neill at the Bureau of Child Care Licensing, Concord, New Hampshire; Pat Moffett at The Nesting Company, Rancho Palos Verdes, California; Torelli/Durrett of Berkeley, California; and Rachel O'Brien, Neta Pierce, Janet Read, Cassandra Wilkins, Reba Kaushansky, Mari Kennedy, and Chris Byrne.

Contents

Introduction 1

CHAPTER 1   Laying a Foundation for Living and Learning 11

CHAPTER 2   Creating Connections and a Sense of Belonging 21

CHAPTER 3   Keeping Space Flexible and Materials Open-Ended 55

CHAPTER 4   Designing Natural Environments That Engage Our Senses 93

CHAPTER 5   Provoking Wonder, Curiosity, and Intellectual Engagement 121

CHAPTER 6   Engaging Children in Symbolic Representation, Literacy,
            and the Visual Arts 149

CHAPTER 7   Enhancing Children's Use of the Environment 177

CHAPTER 8   Facing Barriers and Negotiating Change 191

Appendix A   Resources 209
Appendix B   Tools for Assessing Your Environment 223

The Meridian School, Seattle, Washington

Introduction

This book is a call to early childhood care and education folks to reclaim our roots, rethink what we want our programs to stand for, and transform program environments for young children. Our profession is at a critical crossroads. If we are willing to meet the challenge of taking charge of our future, we have a rich history to draw on and some new pioneers to inspire us. The alternative is for children to spend the early years of their childhoods in cookie-cutter, sterilized, commercialized settings. The choice before us is one of enriching or diminishing our human potential.

Over the past thirty years the early childhood field has formed standards to help us recognize quality programs for children. For instance, mention the topic of environments and most of us have images of familiar room arrangements with the same type of learning areas and materials—easy to spot when you peek into almost any accredited child care, preschool, or Head Start classroom. We have established professional standards that stress the importance of an orderly, safe environment; learning areas; and materials that are culturally and developmentally appropriate. We have developed rating scales and assessment tools to keep us reaching for higher quality. There is much in our profession to celebrate and be proud of.

However, inherent in most good things are the seeds of their opposites. This concern underlies the development of the book you are holding. Homogenization and institutionalization are sprouting up everywhere in early childhood programs. It's time we do some careful reexamination to see how our standards and models have begun to limit our thinking, and how commercial, if not political, interests are beginning to shape more and more of what we do. Early childhood classrooms, not to mention conference exhibit halls, are increasingly far from our roots, filled with catalog look-alike supplies in primary colors, plastic, and prefabricated games and materials.

We seldom use values to guide our selection of materials or to help plan our environment. Though we give lip service to early childhood programs being a home away from home and continually use the term "developmentally appropriate," our programs increasingly feel like schools or standardized institutions. True, we don't have children sitting at little desks, but we regulate their time and routines, remind them of the rules, and surround them with uniform learning materials. We may not ring bells or have long hallways to walk down, but our programs for young children are organized around schedules, standards, checklists, and assessment tools. A more expansive vision for childhood seems a distant consideration.

Finding Inspiration from Early Pioneers

If we take the time to study the forebears (Friedrich Froebel, Maria Montessori, Caroline Pratt, Patty Smith Hill, Rudolf Steiner, and others) who laid the foundation for early care and education program environments, we find important concepts that are seldom referred to by today's practitioners, outside of specialized child development circles. Perhaps this is because we can see their limitations and the legitimate criticisms leveled at some of these early thinkers. Each of them came out of a particular historical context and cultural setting. Their work had internal contradictions, and controversy surrounded them. *Designs for Living and Learning* doesn't advocate any strict philosophical stance or endorse a single theoretician; we acknowledge an eclectic set of influences. Despite the limitations to their thinking, there is much we can learn from these pioneers.

Toward the end of the nineteenth century several important educators began challenging the notion of sterile, passive classroom environments and launched a movement for children to have hands-on learning materials and experiences. German educator Friedrich Froebel, referred to as "the father of kindergarten," launched a far reaching revolution in early childhood education by offering physical objects to children as the basis of their learning. He designed blocks and a series of "gifts and occupations" as part of a systematic method for teaching children through manipulatives. We agree with the criticism that his approach was too structured and limited children's self-initiated engagement. However, our idea of offering children aesthetically pleasing manipulative materials as "invitations to learning" has its roots in Froebel's idea of presenting learning materials as gifts.

Maria Montessori, Caroline Pratt, and Patty Smith Hill were critics of Froebel, but they certainly built on his ideas, as we have built on theirs. We have Montessori to thank for the concept of child-size furnishings and materials arranged with attention to order, aesthetics, and sensory exploration. Hill's recognition of children's need for big body activity and social experiences led to the creation of larger wooden blocks for their play, a staple of any early childhood program. Pratt further extended the idea of block play by developing sets of unit blocks with accompanying props. She suggested supplying programs with an abundance of basic, open-ended materials and ample space to independently and cooperatively explore and create with them. Our profession is indebted to the early schools and practitioners who first popularized these ideas, notably Harriet Johnson and Lucy Sprague Mitchell, the City and Country School, and the Bank Street School for Children in New York City.

People familiar with the Waldorf Schools founded by Rudolf Steiner may also see shades of that influence in *Designs for Living and Learning*. Steiner's general philosophical positions are open to question, but we concur with his idea that education should give children regular experiences with natural materials and the rhythms of the seasons. Waldorf Schools have a strong emphasis on the arts, imagination, creativity, and moral well-being. Though Steiner lived a century ago, we concur with his critique of setting up schools to meet economic needs, rather than the needs of children.

Learning from Contemporary Pioneers

As graduate students at Pacific Oaks College in the 1980s, we were fortunate to be mentored by Elizabeth Prescott and Elizabeth Jones, who pioneered early thinking about creating homelike settings for full-time child care programs. Early on, we made use of the critical components they outlined for program settings, and we are indebted to their ideas about environments, materials, and the importance of observing children's play for our own learning.

Two other significant players and organizations in the adoption of child-centered environments and materials in early childhood programs are Diane Trister Dodge and her Creative Curriculum associates at Teaching Strategies, Inc., and David Weikart and his colleagues at the High/Scope Foundation. While Teaching Strategies and High/Scope each have different curriculum elements and emphases, both approach children as active, hands-on learners who benefit from an attractive, orderly room arrangement, with an array of materials for children to select and use in open-ended ways. Because of the widespread work of Dodge, Weikart, and their associates, the early childhood field has moved away from a more scattered, informal "toy box" approach, to classrooms with different interest areas or learning centers, each stocked with well-organized materials in labeled baskets on shelves. Long before we heard the Italians of the schools of Reggio Emilia refer to "the environment as the third teacher," Dodge and Weikart had set up training programs and demonstration classrooms to show teachers how to accomplish this. Their work has helped to make developmentally appropriate environments, routines, and approaches to assessment practical, and provided a foundation for implementing the ideas in *Designs for Living and Learning.*

Leslie Williams and Yvonne De Gaetano's book, *Alerta: A Multicultural, Bilingual Approach to Teaching Young Children,* showed us how to move away from a superficial multicultural approach and toward cultural relevancy in setting up environments for children. They emphasized the need to reflect the lives and communities of the children and families in teaching environments, which has pushed us to develop concrete strategies to that end. Other pioneers who stressed the importance of cultural relevancy in the social-emotional environment include Carol Brunson Day, Louise Derman-Sparks, Janet Gonzales, Janice Hale, Lily Wong Filmore, and Ronald Lally. The influence they have had on our work is deep and lasting.

Though we never met her, the late Anita Rui Olds is one of the strongest contemporary influences on the program environments that inspire us today. Trained as a social psychologist, and self-taught in architecture and interior design, she taught others how to create environments for children that comfort, heal, and inspire them. For a number of years Olds conducted classes and seminars that provided adults with the experiential evidence and practical guidelines to create spaces that draw the most power out of children. She urged our profession to reconsider design elements often deemed luxuries and claim them as necessities. We are indebted to her fierceness in reminding us that we should be creating sacred spaces for children and planning for miracles, not minimums. Personally and professionally, Olds has laid the tracks for many future pioneers.

Jim Greenman was the first colleague we encountered who consistently used the term "places for childhood" as a mandate for our early learning environments. His book, *Caring Places, Learning Spaces,* is an exemplary resource, in both conceptual and practical terms. For the last decade it has been the primary reference point for the college courses we teach and the consulting we do. His handbook for infant and toddler programming, *Prime Times,* coauthored with Anne

Stonehouse, promises to have a long-lasting impact as well. Greenman also has been involved in the design of many fine early childhood buildings and playgrounds.

The schools and educators of Reggio Emilia, Italy, have had a profound influence in helping our profession rethink what we are doing for children. They have challenged us to reexamine every inch of our environments for the messages they convey. By reminding us that it is not only the *needs* of children we should be considering, but the *rights* of children, these Italian educators have helped us transform our starting place when thinking about spaces for children. Their hard, hard work of building a dream out of the ashes of a war-torn country emerging from fascism should humble professionals in this country when we offer excuses for our lack of will in facing down budget and policy limitations or litigation-driven constraints. The pioneers of Reggio Emilia were sharp-sighted in understanding the real meaning of homeland security, and they pressed forward with a vision that now gives early childhood educators around the world a living model to visit and learn from. Because of their generosity of time, spirit, and resources, many programs in North America are redesigning their environments and programs with inspiration from Reggio. They, too, are modern-day pioneers, and visiting some of these programs has influenced our thinking.

Quietly, behind the scenes, in cities and conferences across the United States, Edgar Klugman, Walter Drew, and a cadre of "play caucus" professionals and folks from educational-recyclables centers have been providing early childhood educators with firsthand experiences of the value of playing with open-ended materials. They have touched thousands of teachers who have, in turn, changed their thinking and practice in providing beautiful, open-ended materials to children. (Plus, their recycling has done good for the planet.) You'll see many examples of what can be found at these recyclables centers throughout the pages of this book.

We confess that one of the major shortcomings in our own professional development has been the lopsided focus on indoor environments. We are strong believers in the value of outdoor spaces for children, but we are more limited in our knowledge of their historical development. We find adventure play yards very harmonious with our values. We celebrate the use of landscaping to keep kids connected to the natural world and the experience of feeling powerful in their bodies. As we've come across these or other innovative ideas, we've tried to include them either in the photos or in appendix A. Clearly there have been pioneers in the area of outdoor spaces for children's programs; we regret that we cannot cite them.

Likewise, the reader will discover that our primary emphasis in this book is on normally developing preschool-age children, though we have included some specific examples for infant-and-toddler and out-of-school programs, and those serving children with special gifts and needs. Our work has been focused primarily on three- to five-year-old children, but we are increasingly asked to consult on the development of infant and toddler programs because many of the same principles apply. We encourage you to extrapolate and adapt if your age group or population is different than one featured in our examples.

Expanding Our Vision of What Is Possible

We have spent the last eight or so years traveling the United States (and a few other countries) as authors, college instructors, speakers, and program consultants, bringing words and images of inspiration and experiential activities. We hope to convey a sense of gratitude and pride in our profession, along with strong words of caution and concern. The emphasis on standards, assessments, and adopted curriculums is often overshadowing the children, families, and staff in our programs because there is a tendency to apply them narrowly without careful, creative thinking. Our programs have been developing what author and Harvard educator Tony Wagner calls "a culture of compliance" aimed at minimums, not dreams, for children and ourselves.

If we embrace the idea of the environment as a significant educator in our early childhood programs, we must expand our thinking beyond the notion of room arrangements. We must ask ourselves what values we want to communicate through learning environments, and how we want children to experience their time in our programs. From the physical to the social and emotional environment, how are we demonstrating that we respect and treasure childhood and the identity of particular children and their families? Are we showing pride in our work and an ongoing commitment to developing ourselves and our profession?

We have received a strong, favorable response to the inspiring photographs of environments we have gathered from around the country. The continual requests for copies led us to develop this book. However, there are always those who claim, "But we can't do that...our space isn't big enough...we don't have the budget... our licenser won't let us." In response to both the nay-sayers and the inspiration she was drawing from more visionary programs, Deb decided to leave her college teaching and return to practicing these ideas with children. She has been teaching preschoolers again for five years now and has learned many things. First, Deb has learned that dreams *are* doable, and they don't require an unreasonable amount of money. Taking time, working with extraordinary diligence, and seeing herself as creative and resourceful, Deb has worked to create a beautiful, engaging classroom environment, filled with concrete expressions of the value she places on childhood. Throughout this book you will find multiple examples of the environment and materials that she and her co-teachers, Rhonda Iten and Cindy Haryertz, have offered over the years. Deb will be the first to tell you that it certainly hasn't been easy, but she has felt rewarded and reassured by the results with the children.

As Deb returned to redevelop herself as a practicing preschool teacher, Margie continued to work as a college instructor, consultant, and trainer for early childhood programs. She often brought photos and borrowed materials from Deb's environment as an offering of new ideas. Margie discovered that inspiring as these might be, teachers couldn't get far with them unless they had a process for examining *why* they do what they do and for exploring the values they want reflected in their work. It became clear that it wasn't just the physical environment and materials that needed reconfiguring in these programs, but the daily routines, use of time, structures, communications, and relationships that had to be in place if the environment was to be effectively cared for and used. The social-emotional environment is intricately related to what the Italians call "the image" of the child, teacher, parents, and the teaching and learning process. Though we don't dwell on aspects of the social-emotional environment in this book, it is an implied foundation.

Designs for Living and Learning is shaped by a particular set of values and beliefs we hold. It draws on the influences outlined above, the inventive and creative work of early childhood teachers and providers we have met, and reflections on our own work over the years. Children deserve to be surrounded with beauty, softness, and comfort, as well as order and attention to health and safety. Childhood is a time of wonder and magic, where dreams and imagination get fueled, and issues of power are explored. In their early years, children need multiple ways to build a solid identity and connections with those around them—their families, peers, role models, culture and community, and the natural world. Children bring a powerful drive to learn and understand what's around them. They learn best when offered interesting materials, ample time, and opportunity to investigate, transform, and invent—without the interruptions of a teacher's schedule. Children come to us with experiences and skills that need to be acknowledged and drawn upon as we coach them into new learning. They have vivid imaginations and theories about the world, which need to be taken seriously and explored more fully. Children have active bodies and a desire for adventure; they have the right to show us how powerful and competent they are. They have a wide range of strong feelings; they deserve to express their feelings and be respected. Their emotional intelligence is as important to cultivate as intelligence related to academic pursuits. And in fact, the research we read in Antonio Damasio's book, *The Feeling of What Happens,* reminds us that emotional intelligence is essential to academic learning.

We titled this book *Designs for Living and Learning* because we believe it is a mistake to make artificial distinctions between how young children live, play, relate, and learn. Their bodies, minds, emotions, and spirits come to us as a package all wrapped up in an ever-accumulating set of experiences, relationships, and connections that shape learning. Teachers must act with intention to make our beliefs about the value of children, childhood, family, community, and the learning and teaching process visible in the environments we create in children's programs.

Navigating Your Way through This Book

In *Designs for Living and Learning* we strive to take early childhood educators deeper in our understandings and wider in our dreams for our lives and communities. Our hope is to inspire an examination of the values you use to influence children and your work as a caregiver and educator. We want to nudge you into transforming your thinking and environments with a determination to move past barriers. We encourage you to draw on your own sense of design, comfort, and aesthetics as you work with the principles and elements we offer.

We suspect you will be drawn to the beautiful photographs throughout the book before reading any of the text. As you look at the photos, be aware that they can be studied further as representations of particular ideas discussed. In the first chapter, we offer an overview of the elements we feel are important to include in early care and learning environments and lay the foundation for the chapters to come. For this reason, it is worth reading first. You will find some initial snapshots to whet your appetite for discovering how these elements might look in a program. This chapter opens with an assessment tool we have invented to help you look closely at how you are currently working with these elements. If you follow the guidelines of drawing a floor plan of your particular space and then coding it as directed, you will discover where you might need some fresh ideas.

The remaining chapters are organized in a similar way, each focusing on one of the elements introduced in chapter 1. Each chapter opens with "Look Inside," a short activity for self-reflection on the topic at hand. We then offer thoughts and examples of how the larger environmental features might reflect the elements under consideration. These "macro" ideas are always under the heading "Inviting Living" and are further illustrated with photos in the "Inventors at Work" section of the chapter. The photographs come from an array of programs with differing budgets, sizes, age groups, and cultures.

Under the heading "Inviting Learning" in each chapter, we consider the "micro" environment of a program with examples of interesting materials for

children and a discussion of how their presentation is designed to invite discovery and investigation. Photographs serve as examples of how children have used these materials in different settings. At the end of each chapter you will be asked to consider possible environmental arrangements and inventions of your own.

If you make your way sequentially through the chapters focusing on each of the different elements, you will arrive at chapter 7 where we suggest some important ways you can enhance children's use of the physical environment. You will find an overview of considerations for the social-emotional environment you create to support children's ability to work collaboratively and develop a focus and intention in their use of the environment. There are ideas about organizing time and routines, helping children discover and use materials, providing meaningful jobs, and choosing different teacher roles for yourself.

The final chapter in this book offers some tips for overcoming barriers you may face, interlaced with specific stories about successful negotiations among directors, licensers, and monitors. These should refresh your determination to push for the transformations you want to make.

Appendix A is an abbreviated listing of print, Web, and media-based resources we have found valuable. In appendix B you will find some additional assessment tools for reexamining your environment.

As you move through *Designs for Living and Learning,* remember that it is in no way intended to be comprehensive or fully inclusive of all the considerations for creating early care and learning environments. Rather, our intent is to give you a set of values and elements to consider, and a taste of how these have been translated into different settings. The examples here are from programs of different sizes and configurations, some fairly well resourced, but the majority operating with very limited budgets. A number of them are from Deb's preschool room and many are from programs that have undergone inspiring transformations over the years. Other pictures are from places we have visited and have been impressed with, or are photos that have been sent to us by people who see themselves as also being on this journey. Our guess is that you are looking for ideas to further your own journey of living and learning with children. Our hope is that these pages will provide you with plenty to consider, and the inspiration to make your own transformations.

Hilltop Children's Center, Seattle, Washington

Laying a Foundation
for Living and Learning

1

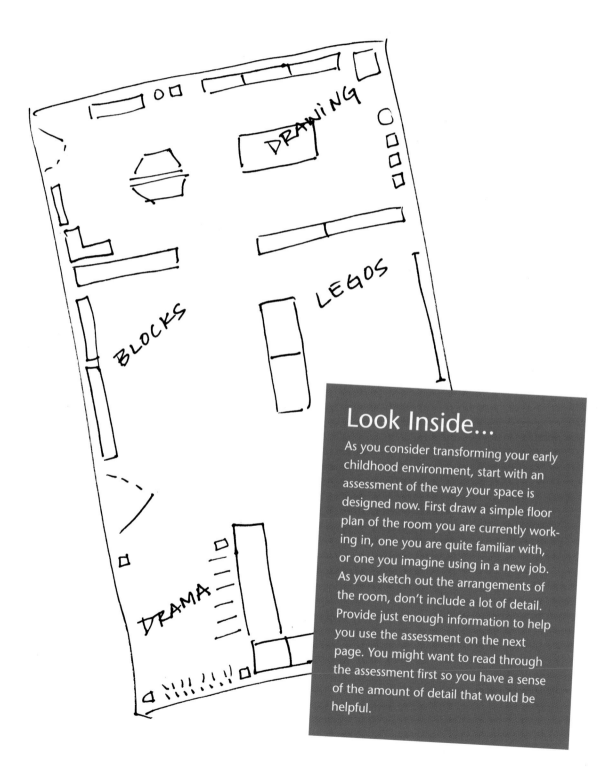

Look Inside...

As you consider transforming your early childhood environment, start with an assessment of the way your space is designed now. First draw a simple floor plan of the room you are currently working in, one you are quite familiar with, or one you imagine using in a new job. As you sketch out the arrangements of the room, don't include a lot of detail. Provide just enough information to help you use the assessment on the next page. You might want to read through the assessment first so you have a sense of the amount of detail that would be helpful.

The early childhood profession has developed many useful environmental assessment tools and rating scales for programs to use in improving quality. However, the one you will use here is unlike the others. Instead of evaluating your space from a set of standards, regulations, or curriculum models, we will help you reconsider your environment from a child's point of view. The elements used in this assessment form the framework of a child-friendly space for living and learning; they will be discussed at greater length in the rest of this book.

The components listed below are geared toward preschool or school-age children. If you are not a preschool teacher, you might choose one of the other assessment tools available in appendix B. There you will find one for family-friendly environments, another for infant and toddler caregivers, and a third to assess the caregivers' and teachers' work environment.

Put yourself in the shoes of the three- to six-year-old children who spend their days in your space. Use the statements below, from a child's perspective, to assess your space. Write the number of each statement in all of the places on your floor plan where you are confident the statement is true.

1. I can see who I am and what I like to do at school and at home.

2. There are comfortable places where my tired mommy or daddy, grandma, or auntie can sit and talk with me or my teacher.

3. The natural world can be found here (such as objects from nature, animals, living specimens).

4. There is something sparkly, shadowy, or wondrous and magical here.

5. My teacher leaves a special object out here every day so I can keep trying to figure out more about its properties and how it works.

6. There are materials here that I can use to make representations from what I understand or imagine.

7. I can feel powerful and be physically active here.

8. I can learn to see things from different perspectives here, literally and through assuming roles in dramatic play.

9. I see my name written, or I get to regularly write my name here.

10. I get to know my teachers here—what they like, how they spend their time away from school, and which people and things are special to them.

Now examine your coded floor plan. Did you have trouble finding any of these components in your room? If so, you will probably find new ways to think about transforming your environment in this book.

Environments Reflect Values and Shape Identity

People in the United States spend most of their time in human-made environments of one kind or another. Some of these are carefully designed, while others appear to have been haphazardly put together. Spaces are typically created with some kind of purpose or intention, whether or not this is evident. Every environment implies a set of values or beliefs about the people who use a space and the activities that take place there. For example, having individual desks rather than grouping children at tables suggests that the teacher believes children learn best in isolation from one another, and values individual work over group activities.

Thoughtfully planned or not, each environment also influences the people who use it in subtle or dramatic ways. Depending on individual dispositions, experiences, cultural orientation, or needs of the moment, people may prefer to be alone or in the company of others, quiet or actively engaged, in bright or filtered light, or in an urban or wilderness setting. An environment may temporarily overstimulate or bore, calm or agitate those in it. Spending an extended period of one's life in an environment deemed unpleasant will eventually exact a toll. Because of this, a number of professional fields focus on designing spaces, from architecture to landscaping, lighting and interior design, marketing, and human psychology.

Children in the United States spend thousands of hours in early childhood programs. Nonetheless, most American programs have not drawn wisdom from those outside our profession who specialize in designing spaces. Early childhood program spaces are seldom put together with conscious, sustained attention to the values they communicate or the effect they have on the children and adults who spend their days in them. Perhaps this omission accounts for the awe that engulfs most visitors to the Italian schools of Reggio Emilia. Reggio programs are housed in aesthetically gorgeous spaces that most early childhood teachers and administrators would love to live or work in. At the same time, Reggio environments deliberately reflect the programs' values and beliefs about children, families, teachers, and the social construction of knowledge. Here's how Lella Gandini (2002), author and Reggio Children liaison, summarizes their intentions in designing spaces.

The environment is the most visible aspect of the work done in the schools by all the protagonists. It conveys the message that this is a place where adults have thought about the quality and the instructive power of space. The layout of the physical space is welcoming and fosters encounters, communication, and relationships. The arrangement of structures, objects, and activities encourages choices, problem solving, and discoveries in the process of learning. There is attention to detail everywhere—in the color of the walls, the shape of the furniture, the arrangement of simple objects on shelves and tables.

Designs for Living and Learning is not a book about the Reggio approach, but our thinking has been on a parallel track with that of the educators in Reggio Emilia for some time now, and we draw inspiration from them (as do many, but not all of the programs in the photographs that fill these pages). The goal of this book is to inspire early care and education programs to consider their values and visions, and the effect they have on the environments they create and on the people who use them. This is not a book about decorating and equipping, rather, it is about carefully thinking through what you believe about children, adults, and learning, and about developing spaces and materials that communicate profound respect for children, families, and the teaching and learning process.

When you listen closely to the stories that adults tell of their favorite childhood memories, you get a picture of an environment in which children joyfully thrive. There are common themes in most of these memories, but sadly, most early care and education programs don't think of themselves as responsible for creating children's memories. In fact, some of the most pleasurable memories of childhood are no longer available to those who spend the bulk of their waking hours in an early care and education program, because of either thoughtlessness or rigid interpretations of standards and regulations.

The assessment tool at the beginning of this chapter uses common elements from countless stories of favorite childhood memories we have solicited in our training. These are the elements we suggest you consider when planning your space:

- Connections and a sense of belonging
- Flexible space and open-ended materials
- Natural materials that engage the senses
- Wonder, curiosity, and intellectual engagement
- Symbolic representations, literacy, and the visual arts

This book is structured around these elements, with ideas about how to use them in the larger features and arrangements of your space, and also in the specific details of the learning materials and how you present them. Here is a brief summary of the elements in an environment that shape a positive identity, lasting memories, and learning experiences for children. In the coming pages a chapter is devoted to each of these elements with further discussion and a range of specific visual examples to study.

CREATING CONNECTIONS AND A SENSE OF BELONGING

Have you noticed that the strongest drive underlying children's daily experiences is the desire to have relationships with others and to be a member of a group? Because they spend the majority of their waking hours away from their homes and families, children need us to help them maintain connections with their homes while they form new friendships and become part of a wider community.

When your environment has a cozy, homelike feel that brings out strong connections among the people there, they will experience a sense of belonging and security. Throughout your building you can create a sense of softness in your selection of color, furnishings, lighting, and materials. You can add specific features that represent the interests, families, and cultures of the children and staff. Indoors and outdoors you can create places for people to comfortably gather, get to know each other, and find avenues for further connections. Providing opportunities for people to collaborate and demonstrate what they know can guide your selection of equipment and materials.

This is the registration and reception area for a large Head Start program. As children and families arrive, they feel welcome in this attractive, homelike room. Notice the objects and furniture that add beauty and softness, while plants and natural light add interesting dimensions. There are also photo displays of the children and families who attend the program and displays of resource materials that inspire the staff.

Karen D. Love site, Neighborhood House Association Head Start, San Diego, California

KEEPING SPACE FLEXIBLE AND MATERIALS OPEN-ENDED

While it's true that children need consistency and predictability, they also need program spaces designed with flexible options so that things can be moved and rearranged for specific purposes. Too often, once a room arrangement has been put into place, it rarely changes. Children are discouraged from taking things from one area to another or playing with material in different ways. This not only limits their creativity, but it also limits the ever-deepening complexity they can benefit from in their play. Children come to early childhood programs with active bodies as well as active imaginations. They are quick to use objects to represent things they are thinking about. Some spaces and materials will suggest dramatic themes that children are inherently eager to act out. Environments should provide opportunities for children to feel the power of their bodies and ideas.

Creating multilevel spaces inside, as well as on the playground, gives children different ways to explore spatial relationships with their bodies. You may envision a loft as a place for quiet reading, but when children are higher than adults, they often want to exhibit how powerful they feel. Rather than subdue their bodies, we need to find ways to help children use them as a regular part of their learning.

The guiding principle is to ensure that there are many ways for children and adults to use the space and materials. Your selections and arrangements should encourage children to pursue their interests and questions, represent what's on their minds, and build strong relationships and a love of learning. Modular furniture that can be turned and stacked in different ways will give you more flexibility than when everything is designed for a single use. Offering open-ended materials in a variety of areas will spark children's imaginations and speak to their desire to continually rearrange and combine materials for exploration and inventions.

Hilltop Children's Center, Seattle, Washington

This room has an open space for flexible use of materials. Children can combine traditional hollow blocks and construction hats with wooden platforms, wooden stands, masking tape, fabric, and tape measures to pursue their developmental themes and current fascinations.

DESIGNING NATURAL ENVIRONMENTS THAT ENGAGE OUR SENSES

Do you remember delighting in the smells, sounds, and textures of the world around you when you were young? It is well known that children investigate the world and learn through their senses, and things such as playdough, paint, manipulatives, sensory tables, and stereo players are standard fare in most programs for young children. But many more sensory-related features can be included in program environments, ranging from engaging textures to captivating aromas. Consider herbs, flowers, leaves, scented candles or soap, shells, rocks, feathers, branches, and pieces of bark and wood.

Filling your environment with aspects of the natural world can further soothe the senses and sensibilities of those present. When you contrast something as simple as a shelf of plastic baskets with a shelf containing natural fiber baskets, the different sensory experience is immediately apparent. There are many ways to incorporate plants, water, natural light, and fresh air into your building. Landscaping should get as much attention on your playground as the equipment and toys you place there.

Because this family child care provider knows the joy of finding squiggly worms, she left this mound of dirt near a cozy, tree-shaded area for the children to explore.

Laurie Todd Family Child Care for Infants and Toddlers, Portland, Oregon

PROVOKING WONDER, CURIOSITY, AND INTELLECTUAL ENGAGEMENT

Do you recall the thrill of discovering a rainbow you created while outside playing with the garden hose? Or trying to find the source of a musical sound that caught your attention when a light wind stirred the air? Children are intensely fascinated with the physical world and how it works. You can simultaneously honor childhood and promote a love of learning by adding different kinds of engaging attractions and discoveries to your environment. This is especially effective when you include things that provoke a sense of mystery and wonder so that children become curious about how they work, where they come from, and what can be learned by manipulating them. Examples include things that play with light and its relationship to color, or things that reflect, sparkle, spin, make sounds, and move or are otherwise transformed by moving air. You can use natural light, air, projectors, and other simple technology to build these features into your environment. Consider various ways to discover and explore the wonder of colors.

Children also love finding treasures—shells, feathers, rocks, coins, keys, flashlights, baubles, and beads. Rotate a supply of these and other intriguing objects in attractive baskets and boxes or as curiosities on a table or low shelf-top mirrors. Create nooks where you can place rocks that glitter or shine, a set of costume jewelry gemstones, or holograms. Putting books, cards, or photos nearby that relate to these objects can further stimulate children's inquiry. Because childhood is a time when the world seems full of magic and wonder, you can keep those brain pathways growing and expanding by placing intriguing discoveries in your environment.

Offering a variety of transparent materials with overhead projectors allows children to explore the world of light and color.

Burlington Little School, Burlington, Washington

ENGAGING CHILDREN IN SYMBOLIC REPRESENTATION, LITERACY, AND THE VISUAL ARTS

Early literacy has become a focus for most early care and education programs, and it is typical to see a selection of books, computers, markers, paper, signs, and labels in designated areas. But children don't just need a print-rich environment, they need multiple opportunities to witness and participate in the process of reading and writing, for pleasure as well as for specific functions. Beyond the limited notions of reading and writing materials for our classrooms, you can consider a wide range of other materials including magazines and newspapers, charts, diagrams, and reference and instruction books. Early childhood environments need to include materials that support children growing up in a multicultural, multilingual world.

Literacy involves unlocking a system of symbols and codes, and there are many ways you can expand children's experiences with this process. The wider world of symbolic representation extends into the visual arts, and adding a range of materials to explore these will encourage children to understand and express themselves using art materials, music, dance, and theatrical expressions. Early childhood environments can be stocked with materials and opportunities for what Howard Gardner calls "multiple intelligences" or the educators of Reggio refer to as the "hundred languages."

Consider Favorite Childhood Memories of Your Own

As you consider the arrangements and materials in your program, spend time with staff as a group sharing stories of the things you loved playing with over and over again when you were children—a commercial toy for one person, a found object for another.

- What were these materials like? Consider the sensory aspects, the textures, the way they moved, the sounds they made, and how they connected to other aspects of your life.

- How did you discover this material? Where were you? Who was with you?

- How did you use the materials? Did you take them apart or combine them, build with them, or act out dramas and adventures?

- Why do you think these materials sustained your interest over time?

As you reflect on your favorite childhood materials, you will probably discover that they relate to many of the childhood "themes" that are a focus of *Designs for Living and Learning*. As you continue, get ready for some wonderful ideas, both new and dusted off from an earlier time. We hope that you will be inspired by the photographs and the elements they represent. Remember to steer yourself away from the temptation to respond with "yes, but . . . my space is so different . . . our licenser (or director) won't let us do that . . . we don't really have access to that kind of money, those resources . . ." Each of the photographs in this book represents a transformation made by a teacher, undertaken against some odds or specific barriers. When you want to design meaningful environments for living and learning with children, you can't take "no" for an answer. You and the children deserve no less than the biggest dream you can aim for.

Hilltop Children's Center, Seattle, Washington

Bridges Family Child Care, Madison, Wisconsin

Creating Connections and a Sense of Belonging

Mesa College Child Development Program, San Diego, California

Look Inside...

If this was the first space you encountered as you entered an early childhood program, how would you describe your impressions? What specific elements make you feel welcome and eager to know more? What elements of this environment convey a sense of belonging for children and families? As you study this picture, how do you imagine this area being used, and by whom?

Although the photograph above comes from a Head Start classroom, this is not a typical picture of most center-based early childhood or school-age programs. Sadly, the majority of children today are not spending their days in homelike environments with vibrant neighborhoods, grassy backyards, or nearby parks or woods. Instead, children are growing up in harsher, less inviting settings, away from fresh air, the natural world, and in many cases, their neighborhoods and homes. The lives of today's children are filled with plastic, concrete, metal, electronic media, and other materials controlled by commercial interests. Most of us sigh and accept this as a given. But does it have to be? Aren't we who set up early care and learning programs in a position to invent something different?

In the early 1970s when the expansion of early childhood education was in full swing, training programs for caregivers emphasized creating a home away from home. In fact, many programs actually searched for homes and neighborhoods in which to establish their centers. In their landmark book *Planning*

Environments for Young Children, Elizabeth Prescott and Sybil Kritchevsky urged educators to provide furniture, equipment, and materials in an environment that responds to the child. Their suggestion was that hard, institutional, school-like surroundings give children the message that "you better shape up and do what this environment requires." They warned that, especially in full-day programs, children would suffer, experiencing fatigue and tension in such an atmosphere. When we fast-forward to the twenty-first century, we clearly see what Prescott and Kritchevsky predicted. Early childhood programs have drifted away from these early guidelines, with commercial interests and political agendas rushing in to steer us in a different direction. Children are frequently tense, stressed, or emotionally strained in group environments.

Early Childhood Environments Today

For families using early care and education programs, each day begins with a significant transition from home to another setting. If the program is a family child care home, the transition has the potential to be a bit less dramatic in its contrast. If it is a center-based program, the transition is likely to feel more like stepping into an institution, a far cry from home. Whatever the setting, children on a tight schedule to leave their families and homes each morning experience a major shift from one world to another. Eventually this daily transition process becomes a familiar routine that everyone accepts or becomes resigned to. If it is a bumpy or less than desirable experience, children and adult family members typically find a way to tune it out and get on with their day.

The predominant stance of early childhood professionals in response to this strained transition has been to regard it as a developmental stage. Literature and staff training on "separation anxiety" has proliferated, offering strategies to help children adjust to "our" programs. Seldom is there a discussion of the importance of helping children remain connected to their families while they are in early childhood programs. We believe this needs to change. A central focus of our thinking should be on strengthening the connection between children, their families, and community settings, rather than emphasizing separation from them during the long days children spend with us.

Young children come into the world seeking relationships for their comfort, identity development, and learning process. From their youngest years they find great interest in other people and animals. Even very young babies are attracted to other babies, their own images in a mirror, and large photographs of human faces. By the time they are preschoolers, they have become fascinated by watching older children and teenagers. It's not surprising that recent research on young children's development shows that children grow and learn best in the context of relationships with the people and places that reflect their families, cultures, and communities. Research on brain development and emotional intelligence also suggests that children must feel comfortable and secure for healthy development and learning.

Despite all this, center-based early childhood programs typically isolate children based on their ages. The babies, waddlers, and toddlers are in separate rooms, and the two- through five-year-olds and school-age children occupy different spaces with self-contained activities. With each new birthday or school year, children often must leave a familiar space and move to a new room and caregiver or teacher. This practice of shifting children is often explained by children's growing physical needs and the program's economic issues. However, this approach to grouping and moving children creates separations and disruptions that aren't conducive to the relationships so central to building trust and to the learning process.

Children, staff, and parents from the different rooms in typical programs rarely see each other, let alone talk or work together. Parents often view classrooms as the domain of children and teachers, and typically drop their children at the door. Many programs even discourage parents from lingering in the classroom, citing separation anxiety or an undesired distraction from the routines or curriculum underway. Parents are often rushed, have parking problems, and hesitate to take up the caregiver or teacher's time or focus. In the typical early care and learning program, siblings of different ages spend most of the day apart.

Staff members only have opportunities for conversation with each other during brief exchanges on the playground or during their short breaks from the children. Adults as well as children deserve to feel comfortable in early childhood environments. Teachers and caregivers often spend more time in these environments than in their own homes. Working with groups of children is demanding and stressful, and should be mediated with opportunities for genuine social interactions with other adults, as well as with individual children.

In addition, we would do well to reconsider the professional notion that employees should leave their own lives at the door when they report to work. Saying that professionals shouldn't share any personal aspects of themselves counters the important goal of building strong relationships in early childhood programs— with the children, with their families, and with coworkers. Relationships go two ways. To build trust and meaningful connections, providers and teachers must be able to share appropriate aspects of their lives and have something of themselves reflected in the environment. Most administrators want more than lip service given to parent involvement and staff retention. To achieve this, they must create environments that say to the adults, "This a place for you too."

How different most early childhood programs are from the home or neighborhood settings early childhood educators first envisioned! Yet many teachers and directors accommodate the current conditions as "the way it is." They dare not allow themselves to dream of any other options, wanting to protect themselves from feeling dissatisfied, disgruntled, or powerless to change the way things are. But stop and reconsider this. Is this really how you want to be living your life? If there was a different physical and social-emotional environment in your program, would you experience your work differently? Would you garner more meaningful relationships, involvement, and support for your program? Could early childhood programs reduce staff turnover, build stronger partnerships with families, and give children the experiences of childhood they so deserve?

In the early childhood community's effort to be professional and to keep children safe, healthy, and learning, we have used public health standards, fears about litigation, and public school thinking in designing group environments for young children. Ironically, this approach deprives children of a key element for safety and security (and for optimal learning) in their early years—a cozy, homelike environment. Young children not only benefit from, but deserve to be surrounded by softness, comfort, and meaningful relationships in their childhoods. Filling a program with commercial equipment and materials designed only for the size, safety, and sanitation of young children also hurts adult relationships, because it creates an environment that is hostile or neutral to families and staff. In light of what we know about learning and development, and in our desire to show respect for children, families, and our work as caregivers and educators, it is imperative that we shape a different vision for designing early childhood environments.

Inviting Living: Elements of an Environment for Belonging

If children and staff are to spend the bulk of their waking hours in early childhood programs and if this is to support and not further fragment family life, programs need to make conscious efforts to help the people who come together to develop relationships of trust and confidence with one another. We suggest that you reconsider both the inside and outside of your building with the goal of creating a welcoming first impression and an ongoing invitation to deeper relationships. The arrangements and provisions in the physical environment create the context for the social-emotional climate and the quality of interactions among the people there. In these pages, you will find many ways to intentionally design environments that encourage connections, collaboration, and an experience of community.

As the photo opening this chapter suggests, the first impression one gets in a building can set the stage for a sense of comfort and belonging. These welcoming physical elements can be threaded throughout the halls and individual rooms as people move through the space or settle in. To create a climate of comfort and belonging, consider these questions.

- Where in this space can you learn more about each other and create more connections?

- How can children and families regularly contribute to the environment so that it reflects their values, interests, and lives?

- What elements might encourage family members to linger before leaving each day?

- How can you stay connected to the outer world while expanding your internal sense of community?

- Do areas of your environment feel institutional and need transformation?

- Could there be more softness throughout this environment? How?

- Does your lighting and choice of colors work to unify and highlight aspects of this space, or does it have a disjointed, distracting quality?

- In what ways can the environment convey the history of your program and a sense of what you value in it?

Discussing questions like these in groups of staff members and parents can lead to new ideas for creating a sense of belonging and connections in your environment. The vision underlying these questions creates an inviting, inclusive community rather than an institutional setting that belongs to sanitation workers or prosecuting attorneys. Creating this atmosphere generates its own energy and involvement. It doesn't require a huge budget and can be accomplished through simple acts and attention to details.

ARCHITECTURAL FEATURES

The entry and hallways in early childhood spaces can become community gathering places that have the feel of a living room or neighborhood park. In very large programs, a number of these spaces can be scattered throughout the building, creating "pods" or a "neighborhood." Creating architectural connections between rooms is also possible with features such as sliding doors or windows that look into other rooms or into shared hall spaces. Studio spaces with adjoining windows or other transparent dividers can offer quiet, focused time for small group work. The Italian educators of Reggio use the term *transparency* to describe design elements that allow people to see through any barriers, making visible what is valued, what has happened, and what is under way—to make connections on many levels.

FURNISHINGS

If relationships are central to learning and development, then specific places where they are fostered should be part of an early childhood environment. Including adult-size furniture not only offers comfort to the staff and parents, but also creates laps for children to sit on. Programs don't have to spend a lot of money on comfortable furniture; you can find suitable items at thrift stores, in classified ads, and at garage sales. Sanitation concerns can be addressed by using slipcovers that can be easily removed and washed. Seek out couches, love seats, overstuffed chairs, gliders, rockers, large floor pillows, and hammocks. Create a unifying, comforting effect by coordinating the colors of the pieces you choose.

MULTILEVEL FLOOR SPACE

Many home settings are designed with multiple levels to take advantage of available space and create a sense of spaciousness. Early childhood programs can create multilevel interior spaces within a single room for the same purpose. The spatial complexity added to a space through the use of lofts, risers, and ramps creates more options for groupings and activities. Looking around the room from a position of different heights helps children see things from different points of view and experience their bodies in different dimensions. This is as valuable for newly mobile infants and toddlers as it is for older children.

COLOR, TEXTURE, AND LIVING THINGS

Warm colors, carefully chosen textured fabric, artwork, plants, water, fish, and gardens have been shown to create an atmosphere where people feel emotionally and physically at ease. Much of the corporate world has taken great advantage of the research on environmental and interior design, using color, texture, and nature to enhance employee comfort and productivity and customer satisfaction. In contrast, most early childhood programs in the United States are dominated by plastic materials, bright lights, and primary colors. Classrooms designed only with furniture from catalogs serving schools and institutions are often either sterile or overstimulating in their ambience. Adding home furnishings, even for storage cabinets and other functional equipment, can offset this feeling. When neutral colors are used, the children and their work can add most of the color. Attention to use of colors, soft furnishings, interesting textures, thoughtfully placed works of art, plants, and objects from the natural world can transform any early childhood program into a cozy homelike setting.

LIGHTING

Many early childhood programs are relegated to church basements and hand-me-down school portable buildings with few windows or natural lighting options. Overhead fluorescent lights usually hum and glare. A more homelike feeling can be created even in these dismal settings. Using a variety of direct and indirect lighting sources can help soften and define spaces. Clamp-on lights, track lighting, a floor lamp, or a table lamp can be placed near a couch or chair to highlight an area and add coziness to a dark corner. A large, well-lit aquarium can have the same effect. Mirrors hung on walls and placed on countertops can enhance the existing light and make spaces feel larger. Many kinds of string lights can add beauty and whimsy to a room, as well as more light. Whatever lighting options you are considering, take care with cords, sockets, and secure placement. Industrial Velcro can be used effectively under many lamps and mirrors. Having an electrician install additional outlets, particularly along the floor in central areas of the room, opens up many new options for using lighting effectively and safely. Try to have separate light switches for different parts of the room, and make use of dimmer switches to give you even more lighting options as the natural light and the level of activity in your program changes throughout the day.

BATHROOMS

At home, most of us give attention to how our bathrooms look, yet we typically don't pay much attention to this important space in our early childhood programs. Learning to care for oneself is one of the most important tasks of childhood, and the bathroom has great significance for young children. Children deserve more than a stark room smelling of urine or disinfectant for the important practice of toileting, hand washing, and tooth brushing. Add mirrors at several levels to your bathrooms, along with plants and children's artwork. Use these around diaper changing areas as well. Make sure that your adult bathrooms are pleasant and don't double as storage areas for dirty paint cups or broken equipment.

OUTDOOR SPACES

Many of the ideas discussed for indoor spaces can be applied to outdoor play areas as well. Study your space, whatever the size, and consider how to add multilevel areas and interesting textures, smells, sounds, and colors. Use landscaping catalogs to find ideas. Consider allocating more of your budget for trees, hills, sand, water, and durable, scented (and of course nontoxic) plantings; spend less on bright-colored plastic toys and equipment. Make sure that there are comfortable places for both children and adults to sit and converse together, as well as places for large-body activity and sensory exploration. This applies to babies as well as school-age children. Approach your outdoor play space as an extension of your classroom for investigating, feeling powerful, and building relationships. For shade, consider plants, a trellis, or an arbor. For inclement weather, consider some of the interesting tent or canopy designs used by commercial vendors or outdoor event planners. Art, made by children or a professional, can add interest and beauty to your outdoor space. Include interesting tiles or cement creations, sculptures, and fountains.

STORAGE

One of the primary reasons early childhood programs look cluttered, chaotic, and uninviting is because there isn't adequate storage space, indoors or out. With limited square footage for a building or play lot, it is often tempting to shortchange storage. The results can have the opposite effect of what is intended, with usable space taken up by supplies, broken equipment, or miscellaneous items with no designated home. In her seminal work, *The Child Care Design Guide,* Anita Olds developed an extensive chart of all the storage needs of a typical early care and education program. This is well worth studying if you are doing any redesign work. Storage options can be creative and attractive. Both indoors and outdoors, you can often develop storage space that doubles as some other architectural feature or furniture element. If our programs are to be attractive and comfortable, we need to have out-of-sight places for extra equipment, supplies, appliances, tools, and things that need repair. These areas need to be well organized and accessible to the busy staff.

Inventors at Work

Programs across the country are reinventing homelike environments where children and adults spend their days living and learning together. Study these examples and consider how you could build some of the elements into your program.

To create a cozier feeling in a rural preschool classroom with high ceilings, the teachers brought in an inexpensive canvas gazebo. It helps define and soften up the space.

Burlington Little School, Burlington, Washington

Burlington Little School, Burlington, Washington

In this program the teachers have created the feel of a living room in the middle of a classroom. The area serves as the book area, a component of any early childhood classroom, but it looks more family centered and homelike, welcoming both children and adults to linger there together. An area like this one doesn't have to be expensive. This couch was purchased at an estate sale for thirty-five dollars, and the other furniture was donated by families. Typically you will see parents reading with their children in this area before they leave in the morning or when they return at the end of the day. What better way to invite family literacy than to offer it in such a welcoming setting? Children use the space throughout the day to read alone, to read with a teacher or a friend, or just to relax and feel cozy on the couches.

Child and Family Development Center at New Hampshire Technical Institute, Concord, New Hampshire

If babies spent their days at home, they would hopefully have cozy places to lie and crawl. Adding homelike features to infant rooms, especially with familiar objects, can help build trust and confidence with the babies. A quilt with Velcro-backed squares, cut from fabric or clothing from home, offers babies a chance to stay connected to the familiar while making new connections.

*Hilltop Children's Center,
Seattle, Washington*

Infant and Toddler Center, Pistoia, Italy

A city school-age program in a church basement has a canvas gazebo to define a protected work area in an enormous room, which was designed as a social hall.

When safely installed in areas away from traffic, soft hammocks have several advantages over floor-standing swings: They take up less space and can be hung up and taken down easily. Some hammocks offer an opportunity to rest while surrounded by friends and sounds, while from hammocks, children can watch nearby activities and discover what else is available in the room.

A hand-built, wooden structure was created to define the housekeeping area in a large room with high ceilings.

Notice how in each of these examples the furniture and materials are a mixture of homelike and school items. The plants, flowers, baskets, and pillows all add a warm, homelike feeling.

*Guadalupano Family Center, Chicago Commons
Child Development Program (Head Start), Chicago, Illinois*

To warm up this old elementary school classroom for preschool children, the staff used carpets, lamps, rugs, plants, pillows, wooden end tables, and benches. Notice the sources of light for the room.

New City Family Center, Chicago Commons Child Development Program (Head Start), Chicago, Illinois

Highline Head Start Learning Center Full Day Site, Puget Sound ESD, Highline, Washington

A beautiful Asian lamp placed on a piece of fabric on top of a shelving unit adds soft lighting as well as represents the culture of many of the children who attend this Head Start program.

To transform the space for their school-age program, the teachers added comfortable couches, plants, lamps, chairs, and rugs to their entryway, which also includes children's cubbies. The result is a much calmer transition to and from the program. In their preschool classroom, they used plants, a rocking chair, lamps, and tablecloths to add a homelike feeling to the space.

Martin Luther King Jr. Day Home Center, Seattle, Washington

This inexpensive photo screen, safely bolted to an adjacent cabinet, displays ever-changing pictures of the children and families who spend their days in this room.

Burlington Little School, Burlington, Washington

Visitors to the Italian schools of Reggio Emilia have been either thrilled or horrified by the "nests" some of the infant-toddler rooms use instead of cribs. Exploring your reaction gives you a chance to assess your image of babies and the message you want to communicate to them. Do you want their mobility and transition to and from napping to be dependent on adult decisions and availability, or do you want to trust them to take care of this process independently? (For a U.S. source of these nests, see The Nesting Company in appendix A.)

Courtesy of The Nesting Company

The babies in this space have a soft, cozy area where they can rest or crawl around, alone or with others. Protected from the larger classroom area, it can also be used for small-group relationship-building experiences between the babies, or between a few infants and a caregiver. Notice the opportunities for the babies to crawl to a higher level and, at the landing, look through a Plexiglas floor to see things from on high.

Infant Toddler Center, Pasadena, California

This caregiver wanted to create an outdoor area that has the feel of a cozy backyard, rather than a school playground. With small hills, large plantings, and an arbor swing, she has created numerous places for the babies to investigate, romp and be active, or to sit and laze around, alone or with a friend.

Laurie Todd Family Child Care for Infants and Toddlers, Portland, Oregon

Transforming a large industrial space, this program has softened the high ceilings and glaring lights with a garden trellis and home furnishings such as a dining table, a desk, and lamps. Strings of lights on the trellis add to the soft lighting and inviting atmosphere.

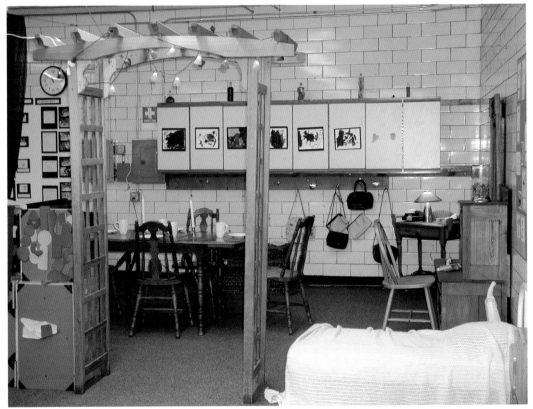

Guadalupano Family Center, Chicago Commons Child Development Program (Head Start), Chicago, Illinois

Here are two efforts to change the feel of an early childhood program bathroom. The first is located in the children's area on the lower level of a family child care home. It features attractive storage and an organized diaper-changing area.

Children First, Durham, North Carolina

In this urban Head Start program, the teacher has hung bead curtains as doors to the toilet stalls.

Karen D. Love site, Neighborhood House Association
Head Start, San Diego, California

In the hallway of this old school building, the institutional feel is softened with a park bench, a lamp, and a display board depicting the lives of the families and children in the school.

Taylor House, Chicago Commons Child Development Program (Head Start), Chicago, Illinois

This inner-city program created an entry space that resembles a neighborhood park with places for families and their children to linger in a more inviting, safer environment than their wider neighborhood. A welcoming entryway slows down the drop-off and pick-up routines in this program, encouraging family members to linger with their children, have a conversation with a teacher, or connect with another parent.

New City Family Center, Chicago Commons Child Development Program (Head Start), Chicago, Illinois

Rooms with tall ceilings can be lowered to create a cozy, homelike feel. Fabric that glitters and shines creates a magical feeling for little ones. Adult chairs, color coordinated with stacking mats, offer comfortable places for children and adults to sit. How different this might have looked had the mats been left in their original primary-colored vinyl!

Infant and Toddler Center, Pistoia, Italy

These photos show windows, doors, platforms, and benches that create connections between the children, others in the program, and the outside world. The first features a window that a baby can look through, after climbing onto a platform, to see into the room next door. The second example is from a Head Start program, located in a low-income housing project, that was remodeled with sliding-glass doors between all of the rooms.

Nia Family Center, Chicago Commons Child Development Program (Head Start), Chicago, Illinois

Highline Head Start Learning Center Full Day site, Puget Sound ESD, Highline, Washington

Inviting Learning: Materials and Activities

The materials and activities we provide, and how we provide them, can help children make connections with their homes, other people, and ideas they want to explore. Daniel Goleman's books on "emotional intelligence" draw on brain research as well as social sciences to argue the importance of helping people learn to manage their feelings, interactions, and communications. But long before Goleman coined this term and published his books, the early childhood profession had been promoting social-emotional learning, attachment and bonding, identity development, problem solving, and conflict resolution as central to academic learning. Our profession has long advocated for housekeeping areas with multicultural dress-up and food props, block props, puzzles, books, and songs to help children play out and extend their understandings. With the enormous variety of languages, cultures, families, and individual circumstances entering our programs, we must become increasingly intentional about the materials we put in the environment so that they invite children to have further connections with their families, develop friendships across differences, and see themselves as part of a wider community.

Children's identity development begins at home. As they begin to spend time away from their families, their sense of self and family connections get tested. Children whose lives at home are stable, secure, and predictable generally have a better time of building new relationships than those whose who face poverty, continual upheaval, and traumas such as divorce, refugee experiences, violence, or racism. Early childhood programs can invite children to be themselves, with all their feelings, interests, knowledge, and desires. At the same time, programs can invite them into new relationships and understandings through interactions with their peers, adults, and engaging materials. Programs can make sure children find familiar things in the environment and also pique their curiosity with new things. As children learn the language and culture of schools and other institutions of power, early childhood programs should help them develop strong, individual, family, and cultural identities. Teachers should also plan with the goal of helping children expand their empathy, emotional intelligence, and desire to learn from different perspectives.

Inventors at Work

Children are very concrete thinkers, but they also have fantastic imaginations and the ability to understand things that seem removed from their lives. This especially happens through stories, supported by adult guidance to connect the stories to their own experiences. Materials and activities that help children make these connections include visual images and physical objects. With regular opportunities to see, touch, and investigate, children acquire experiences with people, places, and things that are both familiar and different. They become less hesitant or fearful and more at ease when encountering something or someone new.

PHOTOGRAPHS

Displaying images from children's home and family life in the early childhood environment creates a continuous reminder of the home-to-program connection. These photos can be displayed in a variety of ways, such as plastic sleeves placed in cribs, photo stands and frames, notebook binders, bulletin boards, or hand-made books. Some of these images should be portable so that children are free to move them around and incorporate them into their play or turn to them when they need comfort or reassurance. If the photos are accompanied by short written stories, they invite children into literacy experiences as well. Here are some examples of the variety of ways that programs display photographs of children and their families.

When parents enroll their children in this preschool program, each child brings framed photos of their family for the shelves of the classroom. The children often incorporate these photos into their play during the day.

Martin Luther King Jr. Day Home Center, Seattle, Washington

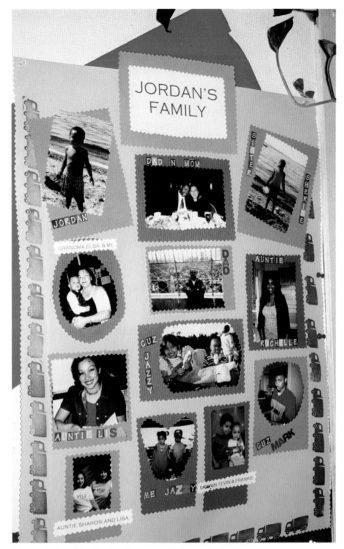

Martin Luther King Jr. Day Home Center, Seattle, Washington

As the new school year begins, this urban program highlights each family on a poster display. All family members are included: aunties, cousins, and grandparents as well as parents. As the children transition from home into the program, they frequently visit their family posters and feel a connection.

This child uses the photos of her family to comfort her at naptime.

Hilltop Children's Center, Seattle, Washington

When photos of the children and their families are slipped into plastic sleeves in pillows, the children can carry them around and to their nap mats for comfort.

La Escuelita Bilingual School, Seattle, Washington

As the toddlers visit their cubbies throughout the day, they can see comforting images of themselves with their parents.

Children's Village Child Care Center, Philadelphia, Pennsylvania

Children First, Durham, North Carolina

Children in this family child care program are continually surrounded by photos and written observations, which remind them of their interests and how they have been spending their time. These displays often spark children's interest in revisiting the activity with the provider, who can coach them to take their exploration further and deeper. Children often integrate these documentation stories into their work, referring to them as the "directions" for recreating their ideas for this next stage of investigation. These visual images and the conversations they provoke help the children better articulate to their families how they have been spending their days in the program.

Martin Luther King Jr. Day Home Center, Seattle, Washington

In this program, family members are asked to bring family photos to one of their first family gatherings. With the photos, they create "family bio boards" to be displayed throughout the classroom. These boards surround children with images of their families and serve as a springboard for storytelling, language development, and exploration of likeness and difference.

A hallway display of staff "bio boards" offers a window into staff lives away from work, allowing families and other visitors to see the values, passions, and influences staff members bring to their work.

Hilltop Children's Center, Seattle, Washington

Hilltop Children's Center, Seattle, Washington

Children First, Durham, North Carolina

In this family child care home, families are encouraged to linger in a comfy chair and read the documentation story books, which describe the life of the program. Then, they can converse about what has been unfolding in the class, as well as similarities and differences to life at home.

Rather than a changing weekly lesson plan, the teachers in this preschool room display photos and short observation stories of the children's pursuits and activities. Descriptions of how the teachers approach curriculum planning and learning objectives are posted above the photos, inviting this connection for the families who read them.

Hilltop Children's Center, Seattle, Washington

FAMILY OBJECTS AND ARTIFACTS

You can invite families to contribute objects to your program that will keep children connected to their homes and help build connections across families. Thought should be given to whether these are intended for display only, or if they are suitable for incorporating into the active life of the classroom. Textiles and woven objects or baskets reflecting the families' cultures add beauty as well as a way to share lives.

Music boxes, musical instruments, and recordings are special objects that everyone can enjoy. Objects representing special interests of the families and staff, such as sewing projects, collections, or games make interesting additions to the environment and curriculum.

Some programs ask each family to bring an object to contribute to the environment. In sunny southern California, one program starts the school year by asking families to bring something to plant along their fence, creating what they call "a friendship garden."

La Jolla United Methodist Church Nursery School, La Jolla, California

Families in this program bring a favorite textile to cover big floor pillows for their classroom.

Children's Village Child Care Center, Philadelphia, Pennsylvania

REPRESENTATIONAL ACTIVITIES

Here are examples of activities and experiences planned by programs to create a sense of community. All of them include some form of concrete representation that becomes a part of the daily environment to help keep the connections alive.

Hilltop Children's Center, Seattle, Washington

Each of the children in this three- to five-year-old room made a self-portrait, working from a photograph. These were then incorporated into a mural for parent night. The teacher asked the parents to gather around and try to locate their children's self-portraits. Parents studied each drawing, which helped them connect to all the children and parents at the meeting.

Hilltop Children's Center, Seattle, Washington

As part of the evening discussion, parents decided they wanted to leave a surprise representation for their children and set about creating a mural of their wider neighborhood, which the children were thrilled to explore the next morning when they arrived. The mural remained on the wall all year and was a regular point of reference for the children's conversations and play.

Hilltop Children's Center, Seattle, Washington

Hilltop Children's Center, Seattle, Washington

Nia Family Center, Chicago Commons Child Development Program (Head Start), Chicago, Illinois

One of the ways this program helped the parents and children become more connected to each other and share an in-depth study was to consider how their hands represented who they are. They took pictures of each child's hands and then at a meeting, invited the parents to identify those belonging to their child. As a follow-up, the children and their parents drew each other's hands, and these representations were left in the program with photographs of the process.

Each year the teacher in this preschool room has the children and their families work together to depict their lives on pages for a handmade classroom book. Each page contains the story of a child's birth or adoption. The teachers, too, add a page with photos and a story of their own birth or adoption.

Burlington Little School, Burlington, Washington

As a way of inviting families to leave a personal treasure of comfort and connection for their children, this teacher arranged a meeting where each family represented their love for their child by personalizing a pottery teacup. These were taken to a neighborhood "paint your own pottery" business for glazing and firing in a kiln. The children then used these cups in the classroom for occasional tea parties. They can sometimes be found studying their cups or carrying them to a cozy place in the room when in need of some extra comfort.

Hilltop Children's Center, Seattle, Washington

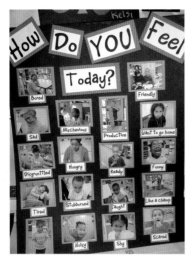

Martin Luther King Jr. Day Home Center,
Seattle, Washington

To help children learn to tell how someone is feeling, this teacher worked with the children to connect feelings with facial expressions and body language. She photographed these expressions and created a "feelings poster." During the coming weeks, when children neglected to notice how a playmate or teacher was communicating a feeling through their nonverbal expression, the teacher would help them make the connection by returning to the poster for a closer look.

Hilltop Children's Center,
Seattle, Washington

Martin Luther King Jr. Day Home Center,
Seattle, Washington

At this church-housed child care program, the teacher told the children that a homeless family would be coming to live at the church until "they find just the right place to live that costs the right amount of money for their family." The children were asked what they thought might warmly welcome the family, and they came up with the idea of making posters and offering toys from their classroom for the homeless children to play with.

As the teachers in this program planned a studio space in their classroom, they took their children on a field trip to visit the workshop of the designer and carpenter. They drew representations of what they saw, and were particularly fascinated by the power tools. Next they visited a child care program across town with a children's studio space already stocked with supplies for project work. Teachers in both of these programs had the children develop representations of studio spaces, which were exchanged, along with dictated letters, and put into books about the idea of a studio.

Located on the second floor of a church building, this preschool classroom had a bird's-eye view of ongoing construction to install an elevator that would make the building handicapped accessible. The teachers took advantage of this opportunity for the children to make connections with the workers. They invented a pulley system to send messages, drawings, and snacks down to the workers; the workers returned notes with stories and pictures of their families. The children learned to tally the dump truck loads using paper and pens kept near the windows.

Hilltop Children's Center, Seattle, Washington

When the teacher in this room vacationed in New York, she sent postcards to the children in her classroom and returned with other visual images and stories about where she had been. Look closely and you will see how the children immediately began incorporating these into their play.

Burlington Little School, Burlington, Washington

This family child care provider always wanted to be a cowgirl and ride horses when she was a child. When her daughters gave her a saddle for her 54th birthday, she immediately placed it in the child care area of her home as a concrete way to share her life with the children in her care.

Little House for Little People Family Child Care, Spokane, Washington

This preschool teacher wanted the Martin Luther King Jr. holiday to be more meaningful than just another day off from school. In the weeks leading up to the holiday, she created a display of books and images representing Dr. King's life, along with a book about exploring skin color and some cloth dolls with different skin colors, and a book about defying the segregation laws in the South in the 1950s. This helped the children make the connection between a holiday, real people's lives, history, and the program's anti-bias goals.

Burlington Little School, Burlington, Washington

Inventions for Your Program...

As you consider your own environment as a cozy, homelike space where everyone has a sense of belonging, what are some of the easiest changes you could make? What longer-term goals might you have? Consider these areas to decide where you might start making some improvements:

- Architectural features and design of floor space
- Furnishings
- Attention to color, texture, and natural elements
- Lighting
- Bathrooms
- Outdoor space
- Storage
- Visuals, objects, and representational activities that foster connections

Once you have defined a starting place, revisit the pages of this chapter related to that element and make some notes. Find a colleague or families in your program to help you brainstorm ideas. Search unconventional stores, catalogs, and secondhand shops for ideas. Move slowly. Each change will suggest others, and it's useful to keep the big picture in mind as you begin to tackle the details.

Laurie Todd Family Child Care for Infants and Toddlers, Portland, Oregon

Keeping Space Flexible and Materials Open-Ended

Hilltop Children's Center, Seattle, Washington

Look Inside...

In what area of this preschool classroom do you think this photo was taken? Is it the block area, the drama area, or the large-motor area? How have these teachers offered possibilities for each of these kinds of play with open-ended building materials, including large pieces of fabric, in a flexible space? What might children be learning if they use the open-ended materials in this multipurpose space?

In designing early childhood classrooms, it's important to designate learning centers for specific child development activities. This sets the stage for the organization of the room and materials, and assists with group management as children learn what is available and where things are stored for easy access and cleanup. Children and adults alike benefit from having a visual logic to the room. However, far too often teachers become rigid in the way they think about and control the use of space in a classroom. Standardization and rules begin to take over as teachers remind children, "Remember those dishes belong in the dress-up area," "Climbing is for outdoors," "Don't build those blocks higher than your shoulders," or "Let's keep our books in the book area."

While we want our spaces to be safe, predictable, and orderly for children, we should be clear about who the room is ultimately designed for—the children's ideas or the teacher's? Children often come up with thoughts about how they want to use materials or space, and in many cases this is different than what the teachers originally envisioned. For example, when six children have begun to work together in the block area, and as a result, the space seems cramped and conflicts emerge, teachers frequently choose to make a rule limiting the number of children who can be in that space, rather than enlarging and enriching the area with additional materials. Does your child development knowledge suggest that children want to do dramatic and active play, construction, or designs work with only one set of materials or in only one area of a room? How often do you find yourself limiting children's indoor physical activity?

Young children bring their bodies with them wherever they go, and their physical development is a critical aspect of cognitive, social, and emotional development. Children need to use their bodies to explore space and what they can do in it—climbing to a high loft, jumping off logs, going up and down steps and ladders, running or riding fast on a pathway, squeezing into a small box, or hiding under a blanket or behind a bush. These are favorite activities for children.

In programs increasingly focused on providing an "educational" environment, the physical needs of young children are often ignored. For the sake of safety and noise control, we limit children's indoor large-motor activity, and in favor of more "learning" time, we further limit the time they have for outdoor activity. Indoor environments are typically designed with areas for small-group play, and "use your walking feet" is a constant refrain. However, for young children (and probably more than we realize for older children and even adults), learning is a physical activity. Young children learn with their whole bodies, in motion. If we limit their activity, we limit their learning. As children spend most of their early years in our programs, we have to continually raise the question: Are we providing enough places for their active bodies?

Of equal significance, when young children are spending most of their days in group situations, is their need to be alone, quiet, or with a small group of friends. Being in loud, large group environments can add to a child's stress, sense of invisibility, and difficulty concentrating. Our environments need to provide restful places to gather emotional as well as physical replenishment. Children need getaway places for small groups to explore their relationships and ideas without interruption.

Perhaps if we initially designed our spaces with more flexibility in mind, we could better accommodate the range of needed activities, and we wouldn't feel so obliged to keep children from rearranging things to suit their needs. This is what the teachers had in mind in the photo on the previous page. Rather than using standard materials in completely separate areas for block play, dress up, and large-motor activities, they designed a portion of the room with open-ended materials that can be combined—logs, hollow blocks, fabric, clothing, and a range of other open-ended props. Notice the portable screen used to designate and protect a temporary space for an individual child to pursue an interest with materials similar to those used in an adjacent group activity. The flexibility built into the design of the space keeps the children's agenda center stage, not the teacher's.

Inviting Living: Elements for Keeping Space Flexible and Materials Open-Ended

When children are offered flexible furnishings and open-ended materials, they engage in the range of activities that foster their development and learning—moving, manipulating, investigating, building, representing, creating, communicating, and problem solving. With these kinds of materials children become more competent in their physical abilities and develop self-confidence and independence. They develop specific skills, self-awareness, and an alertness and respect for others around them. Open-ended materials encourage children to become flexible thinkers and responsive playmates. As you consider how your environment lends itself to these important areas for growth and learning, ask yourself these questions.

- What message does our environment give children about how they should use their bodies?

- Are the indoor and outdoor areas flexible enough to be transformed for a variety of uses?

- Where are the opportunities for individual children to get away from it all and relax?

- How can we create a space where a small group of children can work without interruption?

- Are we satisfied with our balance of open-ended materials and single-purpose ones?

- Where can we add unusual loose parts for children to use, both indoors and outdoors?

FLEXIBLE SPACE AND MOVABLE FURNISHINGS AND EQUIPMENT

As you design your room into learning centers, make sure some of the areas can be expanded when the need for bigger groups or building projects arises. With portable screens or dividers you can also instantly create smaller spaces within larger ones for cozy gatherings or individual work. Two-tiered steps or risers against walls and movable platforms or risers allow children to create different arrangements and scenes. When you provide large hollow blocks in various shapes and sizes, heavy cardboard tubes in assorted sizes, boxes, card tables or other lightweight tables, pillows, and covered foam furniture, children can easily move things around to suit their play needs. Large pieces of fabric can be attached to structures with rods, clothespins, or curtain rings, enabling children to design hideaways and habitats.

CREATE PLAY PLACES AT DIFFERENT LEVELS, HEIGHTS, AND ANGLES

When you vary the space in your program, you literally create an out-of-the-box experience for children. As you arrange furniture, try to create interesting angles and entry points into different areas of the room. An extended platform area in one part of the room, reached by one or two small steps, will expand the sense of space available. Likewise, a loft or two in a room doubles the possibilities for how children can be alone or together. Window seats, the areas under countertops, and closet floor spaces provide other ways to create spaces at different levels.

DEDICATE INDOOR SPACE AND EQUIPMENT FOR ACTIVE PLAY

Children need indoor as well as outdoor places for their active bodies. Consider lofts and ladders for climbing high, logs and blocks for jumping, beams for balancing, and perhaps a rope or trapeze for climbing and swinging as the opening photo of this chapter demonstrates. This large-motor equipment isn't just for children to blow off steam, but rather to develop strength, sensory integration, and a sense of themselves as competent and powerful. Their ability to learn is enhanced.

ARRANGE QUIET SPACES FOR CHILDREN TO WORK TOGETHER IN SMALL GROUPS

Protected areas away from the larger classroom allow children opportunities to have focused discussions and work cooperatively. Studio spaces and quiet coves and corners work well for this. These can be created with hanging fabric or canopies, an arrangement of shelving units, or transparent room dividers made of Plexiglas, translucent Velum, or garden lattices.

LOCATE PLACES WHERE CHILDREN CAN BE ALONE

Nooks, crawl spaces, and seating areas should be available for individual children to get away from the fray of the large group, indoors and outside. You can arrange these with transparent fabric or plant arrangements, which will still allow for supervision. A private place to get away is especially important for children in full-day programs.

OFFER AN ARRAY OF OPEN-ENDED MATERIALS THROUGHOUT THE PROGRAM

You can gather open-ended materials and loose parts, from cardboard recycling bins, junk shops, garage sales, thrift stores, kitchen cupboards, beaches, woods, or parks. These undefined materials invite children to engage their imaginations, see themselves as inventors, and move toward more complex and challenging endeavors. Loose parts call out to children, saying, "Use me to show your ideas and creations." An ongoing supply of carefully selected open-ended materials, some common and some unusual, should be organized and displayed in various parts of your room and outdoor area.

Inventors at Work

Most early childhood programs have less than desirable spaces to begin with, but out-of-the-box thinking will allow you to invent some new possibilities. Try standing at your door, climbing onto a table against a wall, or lying down in the middle of the room in order to visually survey the space from different angles. Imagine you are a timid child, an uncoordinated one, or a group of physically active young friends. How would this space work for you? Study the following examples for a variety of ways to offer flexible spaces and open-ended materials.

A loft next to a window gives the children a bird's-eye perspective on the room and the scene out the window. Notice the use of sheer curtains to cozy up the space yet keep it visible for adult supervision.

New City Family Center, Chicago Commons Child Development Program (Head Start), Chicago, Illinois

This loft has two ways to climb into it: On one side there are large holes suitable for small hands and feet, and on the other, there is a rope ladder. Once on top, children can feel powerful touching the ceiling, or they can cozy up and explore nature posters. Underneath the loft, concepts of light and dark can be explored by an individual child or a couple of friends. Notice the use of glow-in-the-dark stars on one side and a mirror with a string of lights on the other.

Children First, Durham, North Carolina

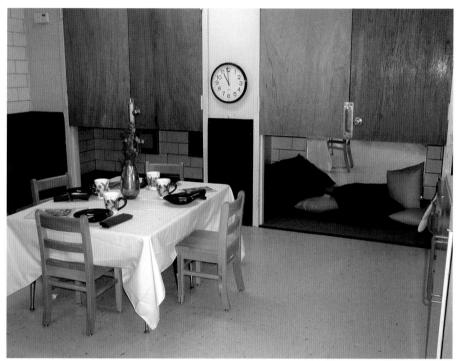

Taylor House, Chicago Commons Child Development Program (Head Start), Chicago, Illinois

An early Head Start program, located in an old institutional building, transformed the bottoms of two large closets to create a crawl-in, cozy place for toddlers. The top of this space serves as a floor for newly designed closet storage.

Infants and toddlers in this downtown office building program can stay on the floor or pull themselves up to the mirror for a look at themselves or what's behind them. Notice the large and small cushions that can be moved around the room for different uses.

World Bank Children's Center, managed by Aramark Work Life Partnerships, Washington, D.C.

*Bridges Family Child Care,
Madison, Wisconsin*

What better or more exhilarating way to explore motion, speed, gravity, and balance than with your own body? This family child care provider has created an exceptional opportunity for sensory integration activities. She so values the excitement, joy, and learning to be found in swinging and hanging that she has dedicated an entire room in her home to a flying trapeze! Careful positioning of the trapeze, padded pillars, and floor mats, as well as conversations with the children, keep this safe and rewarding.

Bridges Family Child Care, Madison, Wisconsin

Risers and steps near windows help babies say hello and goodbye to their families and stay connected to the outside world during the day. The soft pillows can be moved to cozy up any area of the room, and the slide and steps offer opportunities for challenging, active play.

World Bank Children's Center, managed by Aramark Work Life Partnerships, Washington, D.C.

Babies need sensory experiences not just for their hands and mouths, but for their whole bodies. Filling a wading pool with dozens of soft balls invites joyous laughter, grasping and rolling, and sensory integration, along with opportunities to share the experience.

Infant and Toddler Center, Pistoia, Italy

Courtesy of Torelli/Durrett, Berkeley, California

You can purchase these commercially made risers, ramps, and poles (see appendix A) or make your own to offer children the opportunity to design and build their own furniture, structures, and spaces in which to explore crawling, climbing, riding, hiding, and jumping. These materials are easy to rearrange, stack, and store, with a tremendous amount of flexibility.

Courtesy of Pat Moffett of The Nesting Company

A parent donated these cardboard forms for concrete columns as a wonderful open-ended material that promotes physical, social, and cognitive development. Here the children use them to create a partnered rolling game. The flexibility that teachers have designed into the room space also allows the tubes to be used in these more active ways.

Hilltop Children's Center, Seattle, Washington

These wooden stands can be moved around and used for a variety of activities. They can be built or purchased commercially (see appendix A). They can create places to crawl, sit, climb, and hang things from. Here we see how the children have used them along with vinyl gutters, rocks, tree stumps, and blankets to create a cozy house, and on another day, to design an obstacle course.

Hilltop Children's Center, Seattle, Washington

Hilltop Children's Center, Seattle, Washington

Children can safely use a sturdy stepladder throughout the room as they build or try to get up high for a feeling of power or a new perspective.

This program had platforms made to allow block play on three levels. This added more potential for building and allowed the construction to be explored from different perspectives. When not in use, the platforms slide under each other for a one-layer unit that takes up less space.

World Bank Children's Center, managed by Aramark Work Life Partnerships, Washington, D.C.

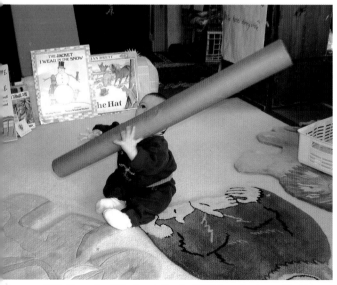

Little House for Little People Family Child Care, Spokane, Washington

This baby's provider set out a long cardboard tube to see how her little ones might use it. She thought they might crawl on it or roll it under their tummies, but this little guy was interested in what was inside and also how heavy it was.

Courtesy of Green Gulch Farm, Portland, Oregon

Here's an outdoor structure made from a tree branch secured safely in the ground. With the addition of large cardboard pieces or fabric, the children have further opportunities for outdoor building and socializing.

This structure was designed to give children multiple levels and spaces for outdoor climbing, nesting, socializing, and surveying the world from up high. In the background is a climbing wall made from recycled tires, built by parent volunteers who wanted their children to feel powerful as well as challenged.

Burlington Little School, Burlington, Washington

An urban child care program transformed their courtyard play area with landscaping features such as trees, sand, grass, and smooth boulders, and supplemented it with a permanent climbing structure. Loose parts such as vinyl gutters and milk crates enable the children to explore height and gravity. Here a water table has been moved near the climbing structure to catch the cascade of water from a hose. Notice that the teacher has secretly added red food coloring to the water for the children to discover before it leaves the gutter.

Universal Studios Child Development Center, Los Angeles, California

Burlington Little School, Burlington, Washington

After observing the girls in her group using artificial flowers, fabric, and colorful tiles in their block buildings, this teacher created an inviting setup in the block area that will encourage their continued use. The girls used the materials to create amazing structures with beautiful elements of design, enhancing their dramatic play.

Burlington Little School, Burlington, Washington

This teacher invited the children to design with marble pieces and recycled clock parts she found at the creative surplus store, by arranging an invitation for them to discover. Before long, the children began rearranging and creating their own designs and constructions, exploring weight, balance, and inclined planes as they worked. Notice how one child created a mosaic of different sized and textured squares, in the process furthering her development of spatial relations, math concepts, and problem-solving skills.

Burlington Little School, Burlington, Washington

Burlington Little School, Burlington, Washington

RECYCLED MATERIALS

An "invention center" or "creation station" is an area of the room supplied with loose parts and recycled materials for children to use in building and creating representations of their choice. Unlike the loose parts in the block or drama areas, invention center or creation station materials are primarily consumables—the children make creations for a one-time use or as an ongoing prop in dramatic play or an in-depth study project.

You can find an array of materials to recycle once you begin scouting for them. At home, collect things like paper tubes, small boxes, food packaging, and film canisters. Some communities have creative surplus and recyclables stores such as those listed in appendix A. The wonderful book, *Beautiful Stuff: Learning with Found Materials* (Gandini and Topal 1999) describes how one program had families collect loose parts for a studio space they set up. This process began an extended project of organizing and displaying the materials, learning about their properties, and then using them for a variety of representations, storytelling, and projects.

Recognizable objects such as bottle tops, corks, straws, pipe cleaners, craft sticks, buttons, wood scraps, and fabric pieces all lend themselves to creative use. Plastic and metal odds and ends spark children's thinking, and the way they use these items often surprises adults. The children use these smaller items to attach things together or create details in their representations. Look for a variety of materials that can be used to connect things—all kinds of tape (including clear tape, masking tape, and colored masking tape), twist ties, wire of all kinds, pipe cleaners, string, paper clips, ribbon, yarn, and pieces of modeling clay. The variety encourages different approaches to construction, invention, and problem solving. Provide tools such as scissors, hole punches, wire cutters, tape dispensers, and staplers to use with consumable loose parts.

For children's representations to be stable and potentially more permanent, make bases or foundations for larger items. Keep a supply of egg cartons, boxes of all shapes and sizes, pieces of cardboard, foam core or poster board, plastic tubs and lids, paper plates, old computer disks, and CDs. Natural materials such as shells, twigs, pebbles, and leaves add a different kind of texture, color, and form than human-made materials. Remember to keep safety in mind when you are selecting loose parts. Watch out for sharp edges and file them down when necessary; avoid toxic materials; remove electrical plugs from small appliances; and follow choking hazard guidelines when choosing loose parts for infants and toddlers.

Noticing that the children had begun making maps to "candy land" and "spooky land," this teacher began to work with the children to make maps of their room and neighborhood walks. Then she suggested they use some of the loose parts in the creation station to create a three-dimensional map. This map stayed on a table for a number of weeks so the children could add props in their dramatic play with it. Eventually it was hung on the wall as a display.

Hilltop Children's Center, Seattle, Washington

These two children were invited to use loose parts to represent the buildings they usually make using blocks. They each took a different approach—one child used only tubes, and the other combined a variety of boxes. As they finished assembling their buildings, the children decided they needed paint.

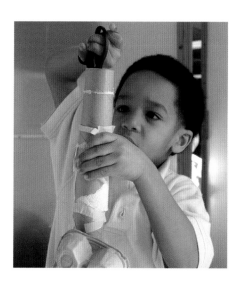

Martin Luther King Jr. Day Home Center, Seattle, Washington

Burlington Little School, Burlington, Washington

To avoid clutter while inviting exploration of loose parts, the teacher at this school stores them in flat baskets that are similar in construction and color. Objects of similar colors or shapes are sorted into the baskets. This display reminds both children and adults that what appear to be throwaway, useless objects can be transformed into remarkable creations.

Without teacher guidance, these school-age children discovered some plastic pieces that suggested spaceships. They used craft sticks to form spaceship shapes and attached the plastic pieces as the rocket engines.

Burlington Little School, Burlington, Washington

MATERIALS FOR DESIGN

Young children are continually classifying, sorting, matching, and transforming the objects and materials around them. With a natural eye for design, they can make good use of diverse, attractively displayed open-ended materials. As they explore textures, shapes, colors, and sizes, they notice how things are alike and how they are different. Children will often arrange items in rows from smallest to largest or group them by color. They pay close attention to filling spaces and sometimes will create recognizable representations if an object reminds them of something they know. These kinds of materials also lend themselves to counting, one-to-one correspondence, and other mathematical concepts. You can intentionally locate and offer materials that inspire children to investigate, design, and learn.

Objects from nature provide an array of texture, color, and shapes that can be used in children's designs and constructions. Collections of almost any kind of natural material, presented to children in inviting ways on trays, in baskets, or on neutral fabric, can lead to many wonderful creations. Here are some suggestions that can be offered both indoors and outdoors.

- Rocks, stones, and pebbles (natural and polished)
- Shells of all sizes and shapes
- Leaves of all sizes, shapes, and colors
- Twigs, branches, driftwood, and rounds and lengths of tree trunks
- Flowers, petals, and herb sprigs
- Feathers of all shapes, colors, and sizes
- Pinecones, pods, and nuts and seeds in their shells

Scout out interesting treasures that children can use in design work at creative surplus, recycle, thrift, or craft stores. Look for items that have beautiful colors and interesting shapes and textures that, alone or in combination, suggest possibilities for classification and order. These kinds of items engage children hour upon hour:

- Beads, buttons, beach glass, and plastic and glass gems
- Tiles, marble pieces, and linoleum samples
- Ribbon, fabric samples, and spools of thread
- Napkin rings, candle holders, and votive candles
- Marbles

Hilltop Children's Center, Seattle, Washington

After playing with these materials for a while in the block area, two girls gathered up the wood pieces and rocks and carried them to the table. They worked for about forty minutes designing a "jungle." The next day, their teacher followed up on this interest by spreading a glimmering piece of fabric on the table and putting a large tree stump in the middle of it. Before long the girls were back at their design work, involving other children in gathering loose parts to add to their complex structure.

Notice how this child explored the concepts of dimension, one-to-one correspondence, and spatial awareness with this design work.

Burlington Little School,
Burlington, Washington

COMMERCIAL TOYS AND LEARNING MATERIALS

Some high-quality open-ended materials are available from commercial early child-hood and school-age program vendors. Choose ones that appeal to a wide range of developmental levels so that they can be used for both simple and complex structures and designs. The higher quality materials tend to be more expensive, but if you have the resources, they are worth buying. Growing inspiration from the Reggio approach, a resurgence of interest in Froebel's gifts, and the ongoing contribution of Montessori and Waldorf schools are spurring commercial development of open-ended, beautiful materials now available at conferences and through catalogs. (See appendix A for some of our favorite commercial vendors.)

You can now find some beautifully designed puzzles and games in stores or catalogs that sell math games and learning materials. Many of these materials can be used by younger children who are not yet ready to tackle the puzzle or game, but still benefit from using the pieces to explore their shapes, sizes, and the ways they fit together. In this classroom the teacher regularly offers interesting design materials on this mirrored counter.

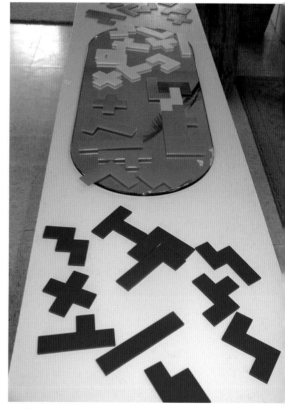

Burlington Little School, Burlington, Washington

Children use these simple small wood blocks to make beautiful designs, constructions, and sculptures. One brand of these blocks comes with a book of design ideas, but children easily create their own complex structures.

Martin Luther King Jr. Day Home Center, Seattle, Washington

Burlington Little School, Burlington, Washington

Magnet balls and rods, called Roger's Connections, can be used to construct beautiful geometric sculptures, which help children learn concepts of math, spatial relations, and architectural design.

Using commercially designed materials based on "Froebel's gifts," this child did some inventive design work—not in the prescriptive way Froebel had in mind, but in a way that represented what the materials suggested to her. This gift is called "Rings and Sticks."

Martin Luther King Jr. Day Home Center, Seattle, Washington

The plastic geometric shapes above, called Wedgits, can be used to form amazing, changeable geometric towers and designs. Toddlers and school-age children alike find them intriguing.

Plastic cubes called Pyramis come with a design tray children can use to build and explore pyramid shapes and structures.

Martin Luther King Jr. Day Home Center, Seattle, Washington

OPEN-ENDED MATERIALS AND PROPS FOR DRAMATIC PLAY

Children find it natural to use open-ended materials as invented props for their dramatic play. Pinecones quickly become food to feed the family. A house is built from scarves and chairs, carefully secured to protect the family from the "bad guys." Through dramatic play, children represent what they see and understand. They recreate familiar scripts to work out issues of security and fear. As children act out their ideas with their bodies or props, they acquire the ability to think symbolically, a prerequisite for literacy and math concepts. They also learn cooperative skills as they negotiate complex play scripts and try out roles and differing points of view. Materials that get incorporated into rollicking adventures help them face fears and feel powerful and competent.

Teachers of young children can enhance this natural flair for drama by providing thoughtful collections of props and materials. Younger children and others less able to use symbolic representation in their dramas benefit from props that look like the real thing. Recognizable props give children a shared experience to play out. But as they become experienced play negotiators and more able to use symbolic representation in their play, it is important to expand props beyond the traditional housekeeping items found in most early childhood programs. Open-ended materials suggest different kinds of drama and offer children opportunities for divergent thinking.

To become a good provisioner of props for dramatic play, it is important to learn about the children's family lives and to listen and observe the children closely to uncover the issues and concepts they are pursuing. Understanding the developmental themes that drive children's energy and eagerness for high adventure, noise, and bravado can expand your mind as well as the space and materials for this big play.

When collecting props for dramatic play, look for a combination of items—objects that come from the children's daily lives, new items to expand their experiences, and open-ended materials that encourage divergent thinking. Here are some examples:

- Hats, shoes, boots, and a few items of clothing that reflect the people and places in the children's daily lives
- A variety of fabric lengths, including fake animal fur and prints, sheer fabric, shiny fabric, ethnic prints, and sequined fabric
- A variety of colors and lengths of scarves
- Capes in a variety of colors and lengths
- A sampling of simple masks
- Ribbon, sashes, elastic rounds, Velcro, clips, and other kinds of ties for children to attach fabric to costumes, habitats, and buildings

- Interesting loose parts that can become part of a drama, including telephones, binoculars, cameras, magnifying glasses, sunglasses, combination locks, keyboards, and flashlights

- Large pieces of cardboard, wooden boards and ramps, tubes, vinyl gutters, and hollow blocks that can be moved and used for dramas

- Boxes, bags, purses, and luggage to be used in a variety of ways from storage to transporting things

- A tool kit and a medical kit with as many safe, real objects as possible

- Open-ended materials from the inventor's recycle bin and other found, natural materials such as feathers, shells, and rocks

Nia Family Center, Chicago Commons Child Development Program (Head Start), Chicago, Illinois

Knowing toddlers like to climb into places, this program set up a tub and filled it with soft dolls for discovery and use in dramatic play.

Nia Family Center, Chicago Commons Child Development Program (Head Start), Chicago, Illinois

In the early stages of dramatic play, infants and toddlers enjoy peek-a-boo and hide-and-seek games. Here caregivers have unrolled a large bolt of transparent interfacing fabric for the children to explore.

Props for drama should be neatly and logically organized, so that children can see what is available and how things might be combined and used together. Placing mirrors near the dress-up props gives the children immediate visual feedback.

Flat baskets or containers can be used to display materials in an attractive, orderly way to help children approach their play more intentionally.

Hilltop Children's Center, Seattle, Washington

As the toddlers in these programs use recognizable but open-ended props, their caregivers discover what the children know and get ideas for other things to offer.

Burlington Little School, Burlington, Washington

Nia Family Center, Chicago Commons Child Development Program (Head Start), Chicago, Illinois

World Bank Children's Center, managed by Aramark Work Life Partnerships, Washington, D.C.

La Escuelita Bilingual School, Seattle, Washington

The girls in her group had been fascinated with "baby play" in the dress-up area, so this teacher wondered if another form of babies might interest the boys in dramatic play. She set up an invitation of natural materials including dried flowers, moss, and leaves, along with artificial birds purchased from a craft store. With photo cards and a book about birds building nests to accompany these props, both the boys and the girls began to develop elaborate dramas about birds building nests, laying eggs, and finding food to feed their babies. They asked the teacher for something to use for making eggs, and she quickly brought them some playdough. Over the course of several days, the children returned to this invitation and at one point began using the book to tell the story of their own invented dramas.

La Escuelita Bilingual School, Seattle, Washington

Hilltop Children's Center, Seattle, Washington

Burlington Little School, Burlington, Washington

Each of these programs—two center based and the other a family home—challenges children to invent and imagine their own costumes and dramas by displaying capes, masks, and a selection of fabric pieces rather than predetermined clothing or costumes.

Children First, Durham, North Carolina

After observing a group of children fascinated with pirate play in the drama area, this teacher offered a smaller "dramascape" using a sand tray filled with rocks; shells; and a set of small pirate props that included pirates, their hats, clothes, a treasure chest, maps, and treasure. The children were encouraged to continue their pirate dramas with new media, changing the scale and creating new bodies for the pirates.

Burlington Little School, Burlington, Washington

Miniature dramascapes are regularly offered on tables and shelf tops in this classroom. Here the teacher designed one with pine boughs, pinecones, herbs, and small bears and deer for the children's play. This proved to be an inviting backdrop for unfolding dramas about the deer family, which was looking for a home and finding food in the forest.

Burlington Little School, Burlington, Washington

OPEN-ENDED MATERIALS OUTDOORS

Children's outside play is a testimony to their curiosity and inventiveness. Even on an asphalt surface, children will search for a hole to poke and prod until they get to the loose dirt underneath. Whether we grew up in cities, small towns, suburbs, or rural areas, most of us can remember what it's like to be a child out of doors. But outdoor play areas in early childhood programs are often nothing but flat surfaces, a climber, a sandbox, and some plastic toys and trikes. Few materials exist for invention, discoveries, or experiments. It isn't difficult to gather a collection of loose parts for your playground. Here are some props that you can make available, keeping a close eye out for safety (sharp edges that need to be removed or covered, and so on) and health issues.

- Large and small pieces of driftwood
- Tree rounds, stumps, and branches—both large enough to climb on and small enough to carry and build
- Smooth rocks and boulders
- Pieces of marble and stepping-stones that can be moved by the children for constructions
- Wooden pallets
- Bales of hay
- Large wood scraps and planks
- Different lengths of vinyl gutter
- Portable ladders and step stools
- Large milk crates or other plastic bins
- Barrels, buckets, and wheelbarrows
- Sawhorses and planks
- Poles with pulleys, clotheslines, and buckets
- Shovels, rakes, boots, brushes, brooms, sifters, and trowels of various sizes
- Spray bottles, hoses, sprinklers, and spigots with water fountains and dog licks
- Pinecones, needles, and seedpods of all sizes
- Measuring tapes, rain gauges, thermometers, and air pressure gauges
- Wheels, tires, and spools

Loose parts on the playground can become a pile of broken junk without a watchful eye, thoughtful planning, and an adequate, well-organized storage system and maintenance plan. As with indoor materials and curriculum planning, setting up and maintaining outdoor materials should be part of a teacher's paid planning time. You can dedicate a portion of your play area to storage of large items, and another area with shelves and boxes or bins for smaller items. Store similar items together for easy location, and regularly discard broken items and clean heavily used ones. Have maintenance tools handy, along with outdoor cleanup supplies.

La Jolla United Methodist Church Nursery School, La Jolla, California

Knowing that children love using ramps and planks, the teacher in this program set up some along with tires, trucks, boots, and a wheelbarrow to create an irresistible invitation. This toddler spent the entire outdoor time going back and forth across the bridge he set in the mud, and up and down the hill he created with the board and tires.

This provider had a simple approach to offering open-ended materials outside. She created a gathering activity for her toddlers by scattering nuts still in their shells throughout the garden; then she gave the children buckets. Their reward after collecting the nuts was to come together for a tasting party.

Laurie Todd Family Child Care for Infants and Toddlers, Portland, Oregon

The children in this group were interested in catching a fairy during their outdoor play. They gathered up the beautiful pieces of driftwood, marble, and other treasures their teacher left for them in the yard. Using these materials, they built a habitat to lure fairies. Notice the jewelry they used, which they described as "swings for the fairies to play on and climb on in case the fairies are too tired to fly." Not only is this construction ingenious, showing the children's ability to take the perspective of a fairy, but it is also aesthetically beautiful!

Burlington Little School, Burlington, Washington

When the teacher brought a large basket of artificial flowers onto the playground, the children took full advantage of these whimsical open-ended materials. A group of children used plastic tubes (another loose part on the playground) to plant a flower garden in the sandbox, and then made bouquets to deliver to friends via tricycle.

La Jolla United Methodist Church Nursery School, La Jolla, California

Little House for Little People Family Child Care Home, Spokane, Washington

This real boat in the yard of a family child care program provides a rich backdrop for adventure. Over time it has become a spaceship, a race car, and other vehicles for the children's invented dramatic play. Notice how the family provider provisioned for more rich drama by supplying a keyboard, recycled motherboards, wires, and a phone cord. These kinds of materials spark the children's imagination and keep their language skills and their minds growing.

Everyone remembers building forts with wood, tree branches, and other found objects, which is exactly how this group of children used the loose parts available to them in their play yard.

Burlington Little School, Burlington, Washington

Children can create "dinoramas" using traditional materials, such as plastic dinosaurs, combined with a variety of loose parts on the playground, such as PVC pipes, ramps, and tree branches.

La Jolla United Methodist Church Nursery School, La Jolla, California

Martin Luther King Jr. Day
Home Center, Seattle, Washington

This program designed their outdoor playground with large rocks the children can use to create and construct. The teacher offered the children an art book with designs made from natural materials. These children studied the book and then spent the morning designing a large, circular mound of rocks. The challenge of lifting and placing the rocks on the pile gave them a sense of power and accomplishment.

Inventions for Your Program...

If you think your environment needs an infusion of open-ended materials, consider where you might find a selection. Carefully study early childhood catalogs or the vendors listed in appendix A of this book. Request help locating creative recyclables from your friends and the children's families. Reading the book *Beautiful Stuff* will give you some ideas about how you might turn this gathering process into a long-term project. As you consider adding loose parts to various areas of your room and play yard, keep these ideas in mind:

- Keep furnishings and arrangements flexible.
- Add different levels, heights, and angles to your space.
- Provide open-ended equipment that can be transformed by the children's interests.
- Create places for individuals and for small and large groups.
- Provide spaces for both quiet and active pursuits.
- Establish an inventors area or creation station with consumable recycled materials.
- Create invitations with commercial and natural loose parts for building and construction, dramatic play, and creative design work.
- Supply your outdoor area with a selection of attractive and well-maintained loose parts.

With this list of possibilities, discuss a possible starting place for you and your coworkers.

Children's Holladay Center, YMCA, Portland, Oregon

Designing Natural Environments That Engage Our Senses

Children's Holladay Center, YMCA, Portland, Oregon

Look Inside...

In this infant program the caregivers created a pumpkin patch right outside their room. If you were the caregivers in this program, what would be on your mind as you selected materials and planned this environment for the babies? As you reflect on the photo, to what do you think the babies might be drawn? How would you describe the colors and textures available here? What sounds and smells would they notice?

If you think back to your own childhood, you probably spent the majority of your time outdoors. Your fondest memories may be of the times you spent in the natural world, scurrying after bugs and frogs, romping with your dog, or building a fort with rocks, twigs, leaves, dirt, and pods. If you grew up in an urban setting, perhaps you scouted for sources of water to play in, gathered sticks and rocks, or watched the clouds roll in or the silhouette of trees or buildings change against the sky with the seasons. Parks were no doubt a favorite destination. The natural world provides an abundance of opportunities to engage your senses. Outdoors you can usually find a hint of an interesting aroma in the air; the pleasure of touching plants, shells, feathers, dirt, and sand; and the sounds of birds, running water, wind, and rustling leaves. With the changing seasons and angle of the sun, you can discover an ever-changing array of shadows.

Those of us who grew up with unending hours spent outside often feel a special connection to the natural word. Our ideal home or vacation spot is probably one with fresh air and views of mountains, sky, or water. Many of us spend our weekend hours designing and working in a garden. In urban settings, community gardens often bring people together, as do their pets—dogs, cats, birds, and fish. We often spend precious dollars on houseplants or fresh bouquets of flowers to brighten our living spaces or to give as a special remembrance for a friend.

Perhaps we seek out the natural world because it keeps us connected to the cycles of life. We continually talk about the weather and pay attention to the changes in seasons. Watching children at any park or beach, we can see that they are especially drawn to the opportunities that the natural world provides to use all of their senses; create adventures; and explore, transform, and invent. And yet beyond some brief outdoor play periods, a classroom aquarium, gerbils, or a water table, few early childhood programs offer children extended opportunities to experience the natural world. With adult concerns about unfavorable weather and health and safety issues, children spend less and less time outdoors. This disconnection from the natural world is an unrecognized tragedy of modern childhood. The good news is that early childhood programs can find an alternative to this national trend.

Inviting Living: Elements for Creating Natural Environments

Whatever your program setting—urban, suburban, small town, or rural; church, school, or portable building; grass, wood chip, blacktop, or concrete playgrounds—you can still surround children with Mother Nature and objects that engage their senses.

As you consider including the natural world in your environment, use these questions to guide your thinking and discussion with coworkers.

- What natural materials are found in our community, yet missing in our program?
- Who in our community could assist us with botanical, landscaping, and animal knowledge and resources?
- How could we gather natural loose parts for our play yard and indoor environment?
- What seasonal traditions or rituals could help children become more closely connected to Mother Nature and the life cycle?
- What sources of water do we have available, and how can we make it accessible and safe for the children's use?

FURNISHING YOUR BUILDING WITH NATURAL AND SENSORY-RICH OBJECTS

It is simple and inexpensive to collect things from nature to enhance and beautify your environment. For starters, try using natural fiber baskets and bushel bins for storage, rather than plastic ones. These can be continually replaced at a nominal cost from thrift stores. Well-placed shells, rocks, and interesting pieces of driftwood or marble can be available for looking at and touching. Tree branches can be hung and large bark pieces mounted as nature's sculptures. Put smaller collections of rocks, feathers, leaves, pinecones, bird nests, and dried herbs in baskets around the building; use good judgment with safety concerns in mind. Young children also love coffee-table books and calendars with photos of the natural world and landscape designs. These can provoke further investigation when accompanied by a basket of natural materials featured in the picture. And of course, all kinds of nontoxic plants in hanging baskets, or on windowsills and countertops, will add beauty, texture, and calmness to a room, as will open windows and fresh air!

CREATING ENTICING AROMAS

There is nothing more off-putting than walking into an early childhood program and first encountering a whiff of disinfectant, urine, or dirty diapers. The power of these odors lingers for a lifetime as our sense of smell is stored in the long-term memory of our brains. You may have had the experience of walking down the street and suddenly smelling something that takes you back to an experience from long ago. Providing wonderful aromas for children is part of building their memories. Consider the smell of bread and cookies baking, mint tea steeping, onions frying, soup cooking, or a scented candle burning as surprise encounters and sensory delights for those who walk into your building.

PROVIDING SOURCES OF WATER

Water in early childhood programs should not be only for drinking, washing up, or occasional play in the sensory table. Water should be made available for looking at, listening to, and touching, as well as playing in and with. It is one of the most soothing and engaging substances that we can offer ourselves and children.

LANDSCAPING WITH TEXTURES, COLORS, AND SCENTS

Before you spend your budget on playground equipment, invest in landscaping features such as hills, trees, edible plants, and shrubs. Plant fragrant herbs that spread quickly and can handle heavy traffic: mint, lavender, rosemary, and creeping thyme can be planted around the grounds, and periodically, bouquets can be brought inside for meal tables, bathrooms, and sensory investigation. (See appendix A for a list of recommended plants.) A river-rock creek bed with a source of water will provide hours of exploratory and dramatic play outdoors. A garden, berry bushes, or a grape arbor offer children a chance to see and pick their own produce before it reaches the grocery store.

PROVIDING NATURAL LOOSE PARTS IN OUTDOOR SPACES

If your playground is mostly concrete and has stationary climbing structures, try adding natural items like driftwood logs, large rocks, shells, pinecones, hay bales, and tree stumps and branches for the children to explore, move, and create constructions. Monitor these items for safety, looking for splinters, thorns, and so on, but let the children use them freely in their play. Look for new things to introduce. For instance, Bev Bos has families bring their Christmas trees in buckets of sand to create a temporary forest in her California yard for January.

OFFERING INDOOR NATURAL MATERIALS FOR STUDY, DESIGN, AND PLAY

Try adding large and small driftwood logs to your block area. In baskets, you can include small branch pieces, rocks, shells, leaves, pods, marble, and tree bark in your block area, on the manipulative toy shelves, in playdough and the art area. Children love to study these objects for their textures, sizes, and shapes. They also focus on sorting, classifying, designing, and constructing with natural materials. Rotate natural things in the sensory table: fall leaves, gourds, pine needles, cones, nuts, seeds, grass clippings, straw, rose petals. Be sure to obtain a listing of poisonous plants and any allergies children and staff in your program have.

Inventors at Work

The United States is geographically diverse; every region's weather is different, and plants and animals in the area vary from one location to the next. For this reason, the work of connecting children to the natural world will change from one program to another. Still, there are some basic elements that most programs can consider, as demonstrated in the following examples.

This block area has been decorated with natural materials collected by the staff and families. Notice how these textures expand the feel of the blocks' finished wood.

E.T.C. Head Start, Chicago Commons Child Development Program (Head Start), Chicago, Illinois

Notice how the baskets and bushel barrels add beauty and texture to these areas; they are also great storage bins. They hold natural materials that children can incorporate into their play.

New City Family Center, Chicago Commons Child Development Program (Head Start), Chicago, Illinois

A sterile, institutional hallway is enlivened by this slim tree branch, topped with a fern plant. Shells invite investigation on the shelves below.

New City Family Center, Chicago Commons Child Development Program (Head Start), Chicago, Illinois

A tree stump and some smooth beach stones collected locally offer sensory delights to the preschool children of this room, and also offer opportunities for design and drama. Notice the book of nature designs that has been placed next to the materials to further spark children's ideas.

Burlington Little School, Burlington, Washington

The teacher in this program transformed an old drinking fountain in their school portable into a work of art. When children step up on the simple rock garden for a drink, they can experience a combination of natural materials to nourish them.

*Karen D. Love site, Neighborhood House Association
Head Start, San Diego, California*

Parent volunteers helped gather rocks for this playground, and a landscape company installed large boulders for climbing and drama. Located in a city with a large shipping port, the playground contained an old boat, logs, and moveable rocks for the children's play.

Clark College Early Childhood and Family Education Lab School, Vancouver, Washington

This family provider landscaped her yard keeping infants and toddlers in mind. The yard has fragrant herbs, different-textured paving stones, and opportunities to crawl in the dirt or search for worms.

Landscaping designed to create varied terrains, pathways, tunnels, and sensory discoveries will engage babies as they pursue their developmental themes while crawling, walking, or being wheeled or carried to this play area. Study the elements developed for this infant-toddler demonstration program, and you will discover a maze of dwarf trees for the children's peek-a-boo and hiding games. A circle of tall pines, with the lower branches removed, provides another place to hide. A grass-covered circular berm gives infants a climbing challenge and direct experience with object permanence (the sand area isn't immediately visible until they get up the hill). A stand of bamboo provides shade and a variety of sounds as the wind passes through the leaves.

Laurie Todd Family Child Care for Infants and Toddlers, Portland, Oregon

Infant Garden Demonstration Program, Center for Child and Family Studies, University of California, Davis, California

Children First, Durham, North Carolina

This family child care program welcomes people at the door with a beautiful collection of shells for children to marvel at and explore. From time to time these change, depending on what the children and families discover as they go about their days.

Nature's materials offer so many opportunities for exploration. For preschool and school-age children, they are especially conducive to sorting, classifying, and design activities. Adding a collection of large rocks, pieces of driftwood, and other natural items in the outdoor environment can lead to beautiful outcomes. Notice how children have tended to both the large and small aspects of each of these fort areas.

Burlington Little School, Burlington, Washington

All of these programs have found interesting ways to have a readily available source of water for their outdoor play. One program installed a dog lick on the faucet, allowing the children easy, self-serve access without the worry of wasting water.

La Jolla United Methodist Church Nursery School, La Jolla, California

Here, a family provider has tied a hose to the climbing structure so toddlers have a water supply.

A hand pump installed in a fifty-gallon barrel provides water in a play yard where no other outdoor water is available.

Laurie Todd Family Child Care for Infants and Toddlers, Portland, Oregon

Burlington Little School, Seattle, Washington

The Meridian School, Seattle, Washington

Martin Luther King Jr. Day Home Center, Seattle, Washington

A water source on the playground offers children unlimited opportunities to have different sensory experiences. Here a sandbox has been designed with a faucet at the far end and a beautiful, curving concrete channel leading from it to collect water. The children can walk or splash in it, float things, or scoop the water out for mixing in the sand.

With lakes and beaches scattered throughout the city, this urban program spent their playground development money on landscaping to create a "beachscape" around an extra large sandbox area. Scattered in and around the area are smooth, ornamental grasses and hardy mint and rosemary plants, which, when bumped into, emit lovely aromas.

Working closely with her licenser to ensure proper hand washing and sanitation, this family provider introduced a chicken coop to her play yard. It provides the children with a sense of delight and responsibility (caring for chickens and collecting their eggs).

Bridges Family Child Care, Madison, Wisconsin

In a courtyard play area, onto which all the classrooms open, this program dedicated a significant portion of space to landscaping with trees, bushes, and grasses. Smooth synthetic boulders create interesting sensory experiences with their different surfaces, textures, and temperatures that change with the weather. The babies especially enjoy these, whether they are crawling or waddling.

Universal Studios Child Development Center, Los Angeles, California

Inviting Learning: Natural Materials and Sensory Activities

Along with sensory-rich natural features in the overall environment, teachers can continually invite children to connect to the natural world with specific materials and activities. Sensory materials can often be changed in shape and form. For example, adding water to cornstarch transforms a dry powder to a sticky goop; tools and molds change the shape and texture of clay and dough; water can be frozen to create blocks of ice. As children work with these materials, they are learning about themselves and their role using the physical properties of their world. Children are transfixed by looking at, smelling, touching, tasting, and moving and rearranging things. These experiences are as vital to young children as eating and breathing. As they absorb the rich sensory information around them, their brain pathways are making connections that will be the foundation for a lifetime of experience and learning.

Sensory experiences are a traditional part of most early childhood programs. Teachers offer children water tables, finger paint and playdough. Sandboxes are a feature in just about every program, and natural materials are typically offered on a science table. Yet many adults limit these activities because of the mess, noise, and spread of germs associated with them. The possibilities of materials and the ways to explore and transform them are unlimited if we open our eyes and our minds to the joy and importance of the natural world and sensory activities.

Are you enhancing or limiting the learning possibilities for children's involvement with natural and sensory materials? For instance, is the same substance left in the sensory tub or tray for weeks at a time with little thought given to the tools offered with them for exploring and designing? Do you provide materials that are already made and mixed rather than allowing children to combine and transform them? Do the tools for playdough go beyond rolling pins and cookie cutters? Have you ever offered natural materials for use in construction, design, and art projects? Do you have beautiful displays in your room featuring natural materials with a variety of textures, colors, shapes, and sizes that children can study, manipulate, arrange, and rearrange?

Turn to your observations of children for ideas, and you will see the many ways they study, design, or transform the materials they use. As children work with these materials, they are discovering their properties and how they can change them. To enhance this investigation, you can look for materials with interesting textures and features as well as tools and utensils.

The presentation of materials makes a difference in how children respond to them. Make sure the arrangement is orderly and attractive and that it suggests possibilities for use. Baskets, trays, tubs, mirrors, or other surfaces define the area and help children focus their attention on what is available. Avoid the cluttering effect of combining different-looking implements and utensils together in one arrangement. Offer sets of things that match and complement each other so the children have a clearer view of what is there and how it may be used. Try offering things at various heights by propping trays and platforms for the children to work on. Here are some examples of invitations with sensory-rich natural materials.

Burlington Little School, Burlington, Washington

When this teacher set the table with a beautiful, flat basket of shells of all kinds, sizes, shapes, and colors, she included round pieces of black felt as the palette for a design. Also on the table was a book with gorgeous, glossy photos of shells. The children examined the shells, picking them up to touch them and look closely. Then the design work began. One child used the felt circle to define her design, carefully placing the shells in a circular pattern, matching the shapes, sizes, and patterns as she worked. Notice the detail of her work, with the small shells in the center of the circle, the round shells tracing the outside, and the longer and bigger shells placed together.

Burlington Little School, Burlington, Washington

Kensington Forest Glen Children's Center, Silver Spring, Maryland

Notice how the teacher has offered a selection of rocks, shells, and corks in muffin tins for the children to do their own sorting and arranging in egg cartons. The teacher's close observation not only keeps toddlers safe with the objects, but allows her to discover their emerging interests and classification skills.

Hilltop Children's Center, Seattle, Washington

One way to expand a sensory experience for young children is to put together some compatible textures and colors. Here the teacher has used colored water, plastic fish, and real rocks in an invitation for the children.

Rocks, shells, wood pieces, bamboo sushi mats, and a variety of combs suggest many possibilities for design work, including creating patterns in the sand with the combs and then lining up the wood and shells. The teacher initially arranged these materials in a tray and then stood back to see how the children rearranged and designed with them.

Burlington Little School, Burlington, Washington

Each day as he prepares the building and grounds for the children's arrival at this Head Start program, Mr. Banks, the custodian, takes time to create a beautiful design in the sandbox with his tools. As the children arrive, they can't wait to see what he's done and talk eagerly about how they might add to it or change it during their sandbox play.

O'Farrell site, Neighborhood House Association Head Start, San Diego, California

Adding rocks and driftwood to a sensory table filled with cornmeal or flour offers design opportunities with added dimensions. These girls used the cornmeal as a base for the drift-wood pieces, which become part of the center design around the rocks.

Burlington Little School, Burlington, Washington

Offering children an array of natural materials at the playdough table can encourage interesting design work. This teacher set out a lazy Susan filled with beach glass and polished stones; another tray holds rosemary sprigs. She also included a set of massage tools, knowing the children would enjoy making imprint designs in the dough. Notice how the red play-dough on wooden cutting boards creates a palette for designing with these materials. This invitation is beautiful to look at and has the scent of rose-mary, which adds to the environment as the children play.

Burlington Little School, Burlington, Washington

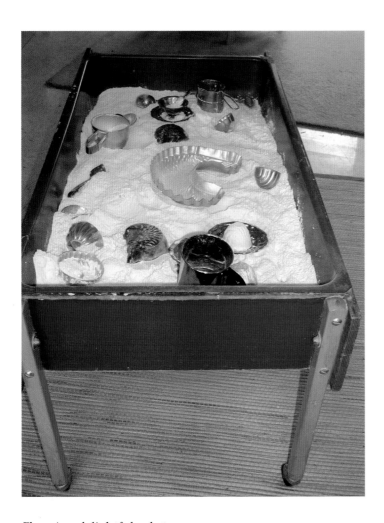

Flour is a delightful substance for young children to play with because it has many opportunities for transformation. These children were offered an array of beautiful matching molds and other utensils to investigate all of the transforming properties of flour. With a sifter, the flour becomes soft, fluffy rain. It can be made into hard mounds and walls by piling flour and patting it in place. Flour takes the shape of any beautiful mold. Flour is soft and silky, a delightful texture on the skin. It turns into a cloud of dust when brushed off clothes with a whiskbroom.

Burlington Little School, Burlington, Washington

This sensory tray is filled with rice and pieces of dried lavender. The sweet smell of the flowers drifts up to the boys as they play. A few plastic jewels serve as buried treasure for the boys to find as they scoop and dig, dump and fill. The children take extra care when they are offered cut-glass containers for their work. The rice flows like liquid through their fingers as they enjoy this wonder-filled sensory invitation together.

Burlington Little School, Burlington, Washington

Rather than providing premixed corn-starch-and-water goop, these teachers understand that combining the materials and watching the transformation is the most intriguing aspect of this early childhood sensory experience. An invitation is clearly organized with a large white tray for catching the mess; the smaller black containers are for mixing. The watercolors and cornstarch are offered in clear glass containers with spoons and eye-droppers.

Hilltop Children's Center, Seattle, Washington

Burlington Little School, Burlington, Washington

Hilltop Children's Center, Seattle, Washington

Burlington Little School, Burlington, Washington

New City Family Center, Chicago Commons Child Development Program (Head Start), Chicago, Illinois

Water is one of the most popular sensory materials for children as it flows, moves, changes shape, and fills an array of water props. Offering water in a variety of containers, and with other natural materials, such as rocks, enhances the experience for the children. Imagine the children's delight when they find goldfish swimming in the rock-filled sensory table.

Water doesn't always have to be offered in water tables. Here, galvanized tubs of different shapes and sizes invite new ways of exploring water.

World Bank Children's Center, managed by Aramark Work Life Partnerships, Washington, D.C.

This display of interesting textures, smells, shapes, and sizes invites children to explore in many ways. Each tray is carefully arranged with beauty, order, and a suggestion for play. Purchased at a thrift store, the materials and utensils are placed on trays and flat baskets to invite focus. One tray has a wooden bowl filled with cocoa powder. The powder can be scooped and transported to fill a double ceramic container with lids; or it can be blown into the air to be felt, seen, and smelled.

The basket tray has pickling spices, which have a strong, sweet smell and come in an array of shapes and textures. Again, spoons and containers serve as suggestions for the activity; the senses are filled with the spices.

The round nuts fit perfectly into the curved bowl of the round spoon. The smooth, shiny surface of the nut is tricky to work with, but after much effort, this child succeeds in moving all of the nuts from one wooden plate to the other.

Burlington Little School, Burlington, Washington

These basket implements and flax seeds invite children to explore textures, motion, and beauty. Once involved, the children find many ways to make the shiny seeds move, streaming from scoop to container and falling through the natural spaces in the basket material.

Burlington Little School, Burlington, Washington

The textures and smells of these fresh sprigs of mint, parsley, and basil beg a closer look, touch, and (maybe) taste. They will soon be incorporated into play ideas around the room that we can follow with the aroma trail they create.

Burlington Little School, Burlington, Washington

Bells placed on a wooden tray invite children to pause and listen to the tinkling sounds. Children compare and contrast sounds, and add their own voices or memories of hearing bells and music played elsewhere.

A pile of dirt in the play yard led these toddlers to discover worms. Seeing their interest, the provider brought buckets for collecting. Soon the toddlers wanted to dump out the contents and investigate. The next day the provider brought an adult-size wheelbarrow and a sifting screen so they could continue their exploration.

Burlington Little School, Burlington, Washington

Laurie Todd Family Child Care for Infants and Toddlers, Portland, Oregon

When he discovered the collection of laminated leaves and flowers that his caregiver had put out, this child carefully chose a leaf, explored it with his hands and mouth, and then took it to the window to show us he knew it came from the tree right outside.

Children's Holladay Center, YMCA, Portland, Oregon

This wispy curtain has more than a dozen little pockets where treasures from nature become visible when the light streams through and the breeze gently rustles the fabric. Children can look for additional objects to add to the curtain or can ask for a closer look at something in one of the pockets.

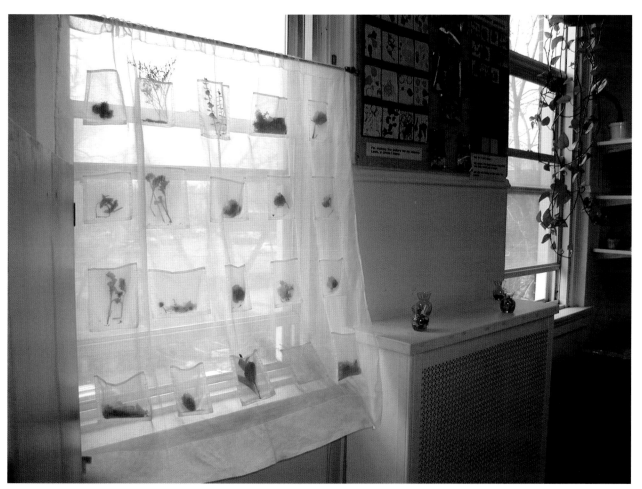

New City Family Center, Chicago Commons Child Development Program (Head Start), Chicago, Illinois

As the seasons change outdoors, a pleasant addition to a classroom is an attractive tabletop arrangement reflecting the transforming colors and natural materials children are seeing outside.

Burlington Little School, Burlington, Washington

In the farm valley where this program is located, fall brings interesting changes in the objects of nature that children see outdoors. The teacher gives the children plenty of opportunity for hands-on exploration indoors. She collects small pumpkins, pods, and dried corn and arranges a beautiful display on a tablecloth with fall leaves and colors. She includes a book about the changing seasons for the children's reference.

Burlington Little School, Burlington, Washington

Spring brings more changes to the outdoor environment, and so the seasonal table changes to reflect what the children see around them. Tulips are in bloom, and bugs and butterflies begin to frequent the outdoor garden in this program. The teacher wants the children to revisit these wonders indoors, so she displays objects that the children can touch, draw, or use in miniature dramas or other designs.

Feathers, pods, nests, and artificial birds and artificial birds and eggs adorn this table representing the birds that the children see in the play yard during the winter and spring.

Burlington Little School, Burlington, Washington

Inventions for Your Program...

Look around your environment both indoors and outdoors for possible places to include the natural world, sensory elements, and living things. Discuss options for care and maintenance with your colleagues. Together visit a garden or landscaping store, sift through magazines, and take field trips to woods, fields, and bodies of water to locate more natural materials for your program. Consider the following possibilities:

- Natural materials, objects, visual elements
- Pleasant aromas
- Sources of water
- Landscaping and edible plants
- Loose parts from Mother Nature (indoors and outdoors)

As with any change, be sure to think through all the issues related to the values and improvements you want to make. Remember to stay attuned to allergies and health and safety issues as you introduce more elements of nature. Also, there is a delicate balance between exposing children to Mother Nature and not dislocating things that should remain in their natural habitat, or suggesting that something as precious as food should always be played with. We want to help children become environmentally conscious and culturally respectful, and sometimes this involves conflicting choices. Ongoing dialogue and research will help you make thoughtful choices.

Karen D. Love site, Neighborhood House Association Head Start, San Diego, California

Provoking Wonder, Curiosity, and Intellectual Engagement

Burlington Little School, Burlington, Washington

Look Inside...

If you walked into this preschool room, what feelings would be invoked in you? Do you notice the light, reflections, and colors? Do particular elements or treasures capture your attention and imagination? Is a sense of wonder and curiosity evoked by what is here? How?

Children are intrigued with natural phenomena and the physical properties around them—things such as light, color, reflection, sound, motion—the world of physics and chemistry. On the one hand, these things are mysterious and magical to them. But children are also eager and natural scientists, full of wonder, observing closely and taking action to try out their theories about how the world works. They are drawn to sparkles and shadows, and attuned to the sounds exuberance, they are involved in important brain development and learning, including the relationship between cause and effect; predicting and hypothesizing; problem solving; and exploring spatial relations, and other physical and mathematical concepts. Make use of ceiling fans and air vents, and rotate interesting installations that offer opportunities for children to observe and participate in the physics of movement.

TREASURES

Providing special objects in unexpected places draws children's attention and focus. Children's eyes and hands are always scanning the environment for something interesting to encounter and investigate. Most of the time when children discover these "treasures" they are told, "Don't touch, be careful, and don't break that." When children come upon something magical, beautiful, fragile, or complicated that has been carefully collected and arranged for them, they know that they themselves are respected and treasured. Special treasures can be selectively hung from the ceiling, light fixture, or doorframe. They can be accessible to children in niches, boxes, and baskets or on mirrors on tabletops and counters. Treasures can be discovered in the sandbox or water table. They are a wonderful addition to bathrooms and hallways. Special caution: Remember safety standards for choking when providing small treasures for infants and toddlers.

Inventors at Work

In a variety of settings, some easier to change than others, providers and teachers are inventing ways to keep children investigating the marvels of the world. As they provide these opportunities for children, their own adult lives have become more alert to and enriched by the small wonders that are part of everyday life.

Plastic beads are strung above a table that has a mirror on top, shimmering and offering a child sparkly colors along with her own image. As the child works with the colored glass shapes, she experiences the interplay of light and color and myriad reflections. The children can also gather the beads together, gently release them, and listen to a lovely tinkling sound as they gracefully sway.

Burlington Little School, Burlington, Washington

Put things in your window areas that shimmer as the light reflects through them. This teacher used a combination of hanging beads, prisms, holograms, and glass bottles filled with colored liquid. When the sun is at just right spot, the prisms cast dancing rainbows throughout the room. The children delight in the rainbows, trying to catch the elusive colored light. You can find these kinds of objects from museum and gallery gift shops, quality children's toy stores, and science and math catalogs. Children can help create an attractive array of bottles with colored water and can experiment with liquid in different proportions.

Burlington Little School, Burlington, Washington

This church-housed preschool room has been transformed into a place of shimmering color and sparkles as fire-retardant fabric and beads strung by children gently sway with the movement of air in the room. Plants create a further sense of wonder.

Teachers in this room created a captivating space by suspending a variety of solid-colored umbrellas from a high ceiling and shimmering glass prisms, which serve as a magical substitute for raindrops.

A sterile hallway in a large elementary school building has been enhanced by little discoveries such as these intriguing treasures that can be woven into a frame of natural materials. A beautiful bench is placed in front of it to sit and study or add to the design.

Hilltop Children's Center, Seattle, Washington

New City Family Center, Chicago Commons Child Development Program (Head Start), Chicago, Illinois

Nia Family Center, Chicago Commons Child Development Program (Head Start), Chicago, Illinois

Burlington Little School, Burlington, Washington

This teacher found a delicate sound to add to the room—a tabletop fountain that trickles water over rocks. The wet, shiny stones are treasures begging to be touched as they glisten under the flowing water.

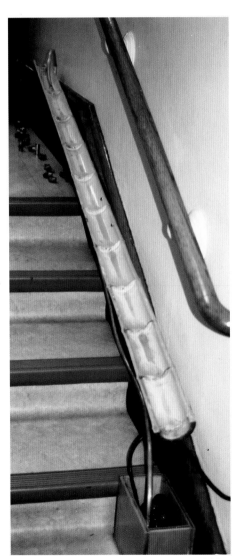

New City Family Center, Chicago Commons Child Development Program (Head Start), Chicago, Illinois

This program invented a way to transform a dull stairway into an intriguing waterway where objects can be floated down a bamboo gutter installation. The brass treasures also make a wonderful sound as they move down the waterway.

Imagine a child coming upon either of these wall mountings, one simple and one complex, but each offering opportunities to explore gravity and sound; dropped balls race at different speeds, zigzagging back and forth across the wall.

New City Family Center, Chicago Commons Child Development Program (Head Start), Chicago, Illinois

Courtesy of George Forman and Weston E. Lord, Loc-Kits, Inc.

Inviting Learning: Exploring Light and Color, Sound, Motion, and Treasures

LIGHT AND COLOR

Along with ongoing installations and nooks and crannies around the room filled with elements of magic and wonder, teachers can arrange materials and plan specific activities for children to engage with these phenomena more actively. For instance, you can purchase or build materials to explore light, shadows, transparency, and color. Light tables or boxes can be found in photography or art stores or in early childhood catalogs. You can also build them for very little expense by studying the designs in the catalogs or by going to the archives of the Reggio e-mail discussion group for designs (see appendix A).

Overhead projectors and shadow screens are also useful tools for exploration of light and shadows. Prisms, magnifying glasses, jeweler's loupes, holograms of all shapes and sizes, mirrored disco balls (large and small), garden reflection balls, color paddles, color cubes, jars and bottles filled with colored water, plastic and glass beads, stones, and jewels—all can be collected from a variety of sources including discount and museum stores, garage sales, and thrift shops. Here are some examples from a variety of programs.

Babies are particularly enticed to experience color and motion with the use of transparent fabric. Here the teacher offered a selection; because the children could see through the scarves, they were particularly engaging.

We Are the World Day Care Center, Seattle, Washington

*Mesa College Child Development
Program, San Diego, California*

Burlington Little School, Burlington, Washington

*Karen D. Love site, Neighborhood House Association
Head Start, San Diego, California*

Teachers in all of these classrooms have created a dazzling collection of mirrors and colored objects for the children to use for exploration, design, and construction. The variety of mirrored surfaces enhances the reflections of the colorful objects and designs.

When his caregiver put a mirror on the floor near where he was playing, this baby caught his reflection out of the corner of his eye. He immediately crawled to the mirror and reached out to touch his image. Imagine the curiosity and wonder as he discovered his own reflection!

Three Dog Family Child Care, Seattle, Washington

Teachers can rotate a supply of materials, purchased or collected, that are well suited to a light table. Painting, designing, drawing, and constructing are all enhanced when light shines from beneath the work. Transparent and translucent objects and paper with color and embedded designs work well. Slides from photos or transparent copies are also engaging. The teacher here offered a set of frosted, lime-colored plastic dishes with interesting shapes that the children used to build and design with at the light table. The structures they create are striking as the light shines through them.

Burlington Little School, Burlington, Washington

Contrary to early childhood lore,
younger children are capable of working with small objects, often demonstrating intense concentration and fine
motor skills when the materials are
engaging and the task is compatible
with their developmental interests.
Here a large sheet of transparent paper
has little doors cut in it, and baskets of
colored jewels are offered to toddlers.
They can try placing jewels in the
openings, which are revealed by
the light table.

*World Bank Children's Center, managed by
Aramark Work Life Partnerships, Washington, D.C.*

A basket filled with folded paper
becomes the centerpiece for toddlers'
small group work at the table.

To sustain their interest, they are
invited to bring the paper to the
light table.

Taylor House, Chicago Commons Child Development Program (Head Start), Chicago, Illinois

This program used an overhead projector on the floor in the long hallway to experiment with light and color. A collection of interesting shapes and objects was placed nearby. Enlarged slides and photos can be projected on the bare wall or screen, and children and their shadows can enter and play in a larger than life landscape. With clear transparencies they can draw their own representations to project.

Children created the enchanting frozen disks of color pictured below. First they put water, colored tissue paper, and sparkly sequins into a pie tin, and then froze it. As the shimmering disc hangs from the trees the children can see the color reflected through it and watch as it melts away and is transformed again.

Little House for Little People, Spokane, Washington

Burlington Little School, Burlington, Washington

Here are two examples of teachers arranging invitations for children to mix and explore colors. Notice how the possibilities are clearly communicated with a different watercolor in each container and with eyedroppers for mixing. One teacher supplied clear ice-cube trays, and the other teacher provided coffee filters—each offering a different way to explore the transformation of colors.

Hilltop Children's Center, Seattle, Washington

SOUND

Offering interesting opportunities for children to experiment with sound keeps their investigative skills alive. It also leads to an intuitive understanding of rhythm and melody that can enhance an interest in music learning. Teachers can provide materials that make softer, melodic sounds indoors, and create opportunities for loud banging and drumming outdoors. Look for sound-making materials that can be explored alone or in relationship to each other. Bells, chimes, and gongs of all sizes and varieties, homemade as well as commercial, are intriguing and, in many cases, inexpensive.

Shakers and drumming instruments of all kinds, including rain sticks and maracas made with a variety of materials, offer different sounds. Metal garbage-can lids and cans of all sizes make a variety of sounds. Consider pieces of tubing, hose, and PVC pipes, along with conventional musical instruments.

These handmade musical structures are located throughout the outdoor play area. The children can be as loud as they like with these interesting instruments. The hanging pipes offer a variation on dragging a stick along a fence as you walk by.

Courtesy of Julie Bullard, University of Montana

Courtesy of Julie Bullard, University of Montana

The teachers in these Head Start class-rooms understand that children are drawn to sound and motion, and they want to provide intriguing ways for children to discover and play with them. In one room, a bench placed beside an array of hanging chimes and bells invites investigation. In another room, similar explorations occur as children hear the wind or as another child plays with different-size bells hanging from the loft.

E.T.C. Head Start, Chicago Commons Child Development Program, Chicago, Illinois

Taylor House, Chicago Commons Child Development Program (Head Start), Chicago, Illinois

These teachers know that adult-size instruments particularly captivate children. In addition to listening and singing along, they love to try their hand at plucking sounds from strings.

Martin Luther King Jr. Day Home Center, Seattle, Washington

Hilltop Children's Center, Seattle, Washington

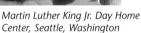

These children discovered a collection of traditional African percussion instruments that their teachers had hung for them to explore. They were immediately intrigued with the many sounds that they could produce.

Nia Family Center, Chicago Commons Child Development Program (Head Start), Chicago, Illinois

In this infant and toddler room, percussion instruments are attached to the wall so the children can use them safely at any time. Nearby photos document children's past explorations of the instruments.

Infant and Toddler Center, Pistoia, Italy

MOTION

With simple props and materials you can invent elaborate ways for children to explore motion and gravity. Balls of various sizes and materials, such as Ping-Pong balls, yarn balls, marbles, golf balls, rubber balls, cotton balls, balloons, bouncy balls, and whiffle balls, are easy to collect and can be used along with ramps, racetracks, planks, slides, gutters, pipes, and tubes, all of various lengths, widths, and circumferences.

Cars and other toy vehicles with wheels of various sizes, wheelbarrows, wagons, scooters, tires, and hoops can move and be moved in many ways. Things that spin, including tops, lazy Susans, yo-yos, salad spinners, eggbeaters, turntables, gyroscopes, pulleys, pendulums, and metronomes, all have interesting motions to explore. Objects that can move using air, such as fans, straws, balloons, balloon racers and flyers, tire pumps, windsocks, air mattresses, windmills, and kites, provide yet another form of energy for motion and sound exploration. Here are some interesting examples.

Taking cues from the children's ongoing fascination with marbles, the teachers at this program went to their local dollar store and bought twenty-five bags of marbles for a dollar a bag. They filled their sensory table with nearly two thousand marbles and added various props for the children to use with them. The tubes and ramps enhanced the children's investigation of movement. They tried rolling as many marbles as they could, as fast as they could, down the ramps and through the tubes, onto the floor, and occasionally into the basket.

The object in the middle of the table is an adaptation of a design from the Hearthsong toy company (see appendix A). It has a series of Plexiglas petals of various sizes attached along the length of a piece of wood. The children release marbles onto the top petal, and as they move down the other petals, they make a musical sound that changes as each marble strikes a petal, like a melody of raindrops. The marbles magically reflect light and color off the Plexiglas as they fall.

Burlington Little School, Burlington, Washington

Burlington Little School, Burlington, Washington

A collection of simple props, such as cardboard tubes and plastic race tracks found at a garage sale, combined with blocks and a variety of balls, marbles, and cars, invites children to build their own ramp configurations and investigate the differences in speed and motion using various props.

After using the plastic racetrack pieces in the block area, these children decided to try something new by moving them to the sensory table. Teachers could see them gain new understandings about inclines and angles as they used flour, rather than balls, as a medium for movement.

Burlington Little School, Burlington, Washington

Inexpensive gutters can be purchased at any hardware store and cut into various lengths for versatile uses, such as building inclines and raceways. Here the gutter has been attached to a rope with a pulley. The children use this setup to negotiate the movement of a ball inside the gutter as they pull it up with the rope and pulley. It's a tricky and engaging task, and with practice they construct the understandings they need to be successful.

Evergreen Community School, Santa Monica, California

This outdoor waterway starts with a PVC pipe structure, which holds hanging flexible tubes and funnels above a water table. The children construct various pathways for the water to travel by wrapping the tubes around the PVC pipe. Then they stand on the plastic bins to pour in the water and watch their theories at work.

Evergreen Community School, Santa Monica, California

This idea was adapted from college instructor Tom Drummond, who created a structure of wire baskets in a water table through which clear plastic tubing was arranged. Here, the children pour colored water into funnels at the ends of the tubes and watch how varying volume and pressure force the water to move through the tubes at different speeds.

Martin Luther King Jr. Day Home Center, Seattle, Washington

World Bank Children's Center, managed by Aramark Work Life Partnerships, Washington, D.C.

Simple and beautiful fans can provide a captivating study of air—how it feels on your skin and how it moves and affects other objects. Many explorations can be made using cotton balls, light fabrics, or air-filled balloons.

Using hoops, pulleys, chain, and rope, this teacher has invented complex contraptions where children can take action and make something interesting happen.

This contraption is an inverted table on which a hoop, attached to a pole, has been placed. The children push the hoop and watch as it spins in its own orbit while spinning around the pole—two spinning actions at once!

The pulley system invites the children to explore how objects move in space and how one action causes another action. As they pull on the ropes, different things happen—containers rise, and the hoop turns.

Helen Gordon Child Development Center, Portland, Oregon

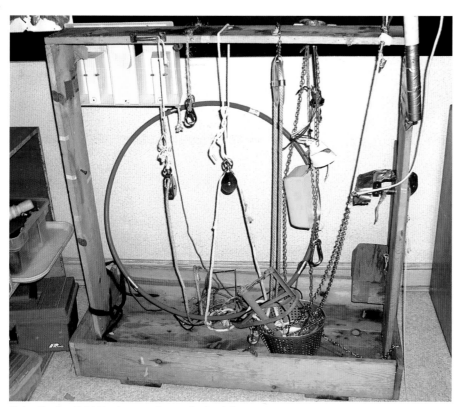

Helen Gordon Child Development Center, Portland, Oregon

TREASURES

Materials that are offered as treasures can include things with interesting textures, smells, colors, sparkles, or patterns. Combining particular materials invites children to explore and interact with them, perhaps touching, designing, building, or learning a concept. Materials can be offered on top of a glimmering piece of fabric, a beautiful tray, a piece of wood, or a mirror. They might be in a beautiful box that children can open.

A companion book or photograph with a related visual image adds to the children's sense of discovery and desire to explore. Here are some diverse examples.

Burlington Little School, Burlington, Washington

This teacher was inspired by the teachers of Reggio Emilia, whose children use overhead projectors. She offers glass shapes for the children to investigate. The light glows through the colored shapes as the children arrange them on top of the lighted surface. Even better, the beautiful design magically appears on the wall.

When color is woven into beautiful little baskets, children are prompted not only to touch and play with them, but also to extend their investigation of how color works in a weaving with other media. As they carry the baskets around, children discover little shells, feathers, or stones that their teachers or peers have put in them.

Hilltop Children's Center, Seattle, Washington

A treasure box filled with a variety of plastic jewels, placed alongside a series of cups for sorting, leads children to days of questions, sorting and designing, and dramatic play with these sparkly treasures.

The children in this program were delighted to discover this unique treasure of artificial flowers in miniature pots on trays. They created and recreated beautiful bouquets and flower arrangements.

Hilltop Children's Center, Seattle, Washington

Burlington Little School, Burlington, Washington

Burlington Little School, Burlington, Washington

Teachers in two programs chose different ways to invite children to explore an interesting collection of napkin rings found at thrift stores.

A collection of little boxes of different textures—some cloth, some metal, some hinged, some with removable lids—creates an invitation for these toddlers to open them and find a treasure. The repeated process of opening and closing, carrying and dumping is enhanced by these unusual objects.

Martin Luther King Jr. Day Home Center, Seattle, Washington

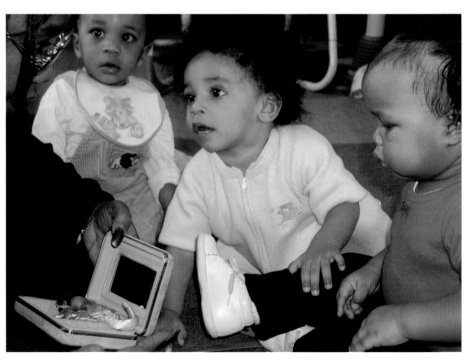

We Are the World Day Care, Seattle, Washington

The babies in this program have interesting treasures mounted on a wall for their exploration. The caregivers attached smooth porcelain knobs that move, along with textured shells and bristly brushes.

Nia Family Center, Chicago Commons Child Development Program (Head Start), Chicago, Illinois

The gauzy curtains, shapes on the light table, and colorful, shimmering fabric set an enchanted stage for the children's explorations and drama in this classroom.

Hilltop Children's Center, Seattle, Washington

Toddlers love to carry bags around. The teacher at this center set out a collection of shimmering bags filled with sparkly ribbons. The texture and sound made these especially interesting bags for the toddlers to continually fill and empty.

We Are the World Day Care, Seattle, Washington

These invitations were created so teachers could learn more about the children's interest in skin color. The different-colored cloth dolls, wooden figures, and books were left out for a while so the children could investigate and discuss. Teachers could observe the children's interactions with the materials and form their own questions and ideas. From these observations, they planned more activities and added materials that reflected the children's interests and theories.

Burlington Little School, Burlington, Washington

Inventions for Your Program...

If the idea of stimulating wonder and intellectual curiosity by using light, shadows, mirrors, and sound is new to you, it might be time for some investigations of your own. Gather your coworkers together and try exploring something like the different ways prisms disperse dancing colors. Put a mirror on a table; on it, build with Lego blocks. Discuss with your colleagues how these small additions enhance your opportunities for new discoveries or enliven your sense of wonder. Begin to notice these things when you are out in the world. Consider one or more of these elements to enhance your environment, indoors and outdoors:

- Working with light, color, shadows
- Exploring sound
- Investigating motion and gravity
- Discovering treasures to include in play activities

As you begin to expand opportunities for curiosity and intellectual engagement, be prepared to build on the interests and ideas that the children generate. This might involve gathering some additional resource materials to have in the wings, and enhancing your understandings of how to extend key elements of the children's investigation into long-term project work. For further ideas, see the resources related to Reggio Emilia and the video listings in appendix A.

Three Dog Family Child Care, Seattle, Washington

Engaging Children in Symbolic Representation, Literacy, and the Visual Arts

6

Hilltop Children's Center, Seattle, Washington

Look Inside...

Seeing that some of her preschoolers were interested in board games and mazes, this teacher gathered a set of art supplies as well as two of the children's favorite games, and invited them to make their own board game. What do you think might have influenced her decision to offer these materials? Once the children are clearly engaged with the materials, the teacher has chosen to stand back and observe what unfolds, thinking of herself as a researcher of the children's interests, understandings, and capabilities. What questions might she have? What in this picture indicates the teacher's understanding about the relationship between symbolic representation, literacy, and the co-construction of knowledge?

With a growing emphasis in the United States on teaching literacy skills, bypassing the necessary stages of literacy development for young children is a dangerous possibility. Instead, educators and parents alike are jumping directly to teaching children the forms and conventions of print and phonemic competencies. While children may benefit from this instruction at the right points in their development, they must first be exposed to the joys of literacy, which provide far more significant impetus to learn to read than the external reward of a sticker, praise, or pleasing an adult. When children are pushed into reading and writing instruction without offering them a context for its meaning, they typically respond in one of the following ways: lack of interest, memorization with no understanding, stress, or rebellion. In contrast, when they are in an environment filled with diverse, everyday literacy experiences, they come to understand its value and meaning, and are then eager to decode and reproduce these symbols in their world.

Burlington Little School, Burlington, Washington

Karen D. Love site, Neighborhood House Association Head Start, San Diego, California

Burlington Little School, Burlington, Washington

Finding attractive ways to offer children tools for writing is a priority for all of these teachers. One has made clipboards with pens available to carry to different parts of the room, while another offers folders and individual journal books for writing in. Writing, drawing, and bookmaking tools are always displayed in an organized, visually pleasing way. Displaying samples of children's writing and photos of them engaged in the writing process stimulates their interest in experimenting with the tools that are available.

Mesa College Child Development Center, San Diego, California

Every day, the children watch an adult sign them in and out of the program, so this preschool teacher decided to have a sign-in sheet for the children to use as well.

Burlington Little School, Burlington, Washington

Wanting to help their children understand that music, too, is a language with written symbols, the teachers in this Head Start program set up a music table with a CD player, discs, and a clipboard with a music score. They invite the children to try making their own music notations as well.

Alhambra Head Start, Phoenix, Arizona

Alhambra Head Start, Phoenix, Arizona

Framed prints and artifacts of well-known artists can be found throughout this Head Start program. They represent both the European classics and artists from the cultural groups of children in the program. In many cases, the children's efforts to represent an artist's style are displayed right alongside, giving them the same level of visibility and respect.

Karen D. Love site, Neighborhood House Association Head Start, San Diego, California

Wanting the children to see themselves as visual artists, this teacher starts the year off with a set of empty picture frames on the wall. As the children create their own drawings and paintings, these begin to fill the frames, helping the children see that their efforts at visual representations are highly valued.

As she scoured art stores for studio tools that would be safe for children to use independently or with adult guidance, this teacher wanted to include cultural diversity in her selection. She used wood stain to vary the colors of the human figure models that she purchased.

Hilltop Children's Center, Seattle, Washington

Using a separate room for a studio space wasn't an option, so this teacher created one in the corner of her classroom. Tall, open shelving units with garden lattices nailed to their backs define this as a separate space, but also give it enough transparency to keep the small-group work connected to the larger group, and allow for adequate supervision.

Burlington Little School, Burlington, Washington

Wanting to work closely with and represent the children's heritages, this Head Start program includes an ongoing display of their cultural heroes, artists, leaders, and role models. The display generates storytelling and opportunities to honor their home languages.

Alhambra Head Start, Phoenix, Arizona

To build partnerships with families in developing literacy skills, this program developed take-home literacy backpacks. Each includes a selection of books and hands-on materials centered around a theme, such as family life, animals, sports, eating, or artists. A tape recorder, a journal, and a camera allow the family to record their experiences with the materials at home. Teachers use this documentation to develop further literacy work with the children and their families.

Martin Luther King Jr. Day Home Center, Seattle, Washington

Inviting Learning: Materials and Activities

Children can have multiple opportunities to explore the world of symbolic representation, literacy, and the visual arts in the classroom. As you watch how children respond to this environment and hear the themes that emerge in their play, you can offer additional materials, or suggest that the children create them, for further involvement in literacy experiences. As you do this, be alert to what children demonstrate they already know; this will stimulate further ideas for materials and activities to scaffold their learning to the next stage.

When she noticed that the children were using the playdough for stamping out letters, the teacher in this preschool program arranged for them to work further with alphabet stamps and charts.

Martin Luther King Jr. Day Home Center, Seattle, Washington

This teacher discovered a child choosing some of the shapes of the letters of his name to put on the overhead projector. This reminded her that it was time to offer that child additional literacy materials and activities.

Burlington Little School, Burlington, Washington

Martin Luther King Jr. Day Home Center, Seattle, Washington

The preschool children in this room build remarkable structures with Kapla blocks. One day the teacher found them doing something else with these thin wooden blocks—creating the letters of their names. Next she had them use other materials, as well as work on finding and representing each other's names.

Burlington Little School, Burlington, Washington

Noticing that her children had been building fort structures on the play yard, this teacher began to provide writing materials so they could make signs. As a result, these children acquired a new interest in writing.

Alhambra Head Start, Phoenix, Arizona

For children who actively avoid the writing center in favor of playing outside or in the block or drama areas, bring literacy materials to these areas, which will allow them to see how literacy is useful. This classroom has a basket of blueprints in the literacy center. When the teacher observed the seriousness with which some of her boys approached their building projects, she introduced the blueprints so they could learn about this symbolic representation of building designs.

As children progress in their literacy development, they begin to make written symbols distinctively different from their drawing. This child's teacher observed that he was learning the difference and invited him to put some words inside his building. Look closely at what he is doing.

Watching his caregiver regularly use a pen and paper, this toddler demonstrated an interest in writing as well. The caregiver then developed a special handled writing box, filled with pens and paper, that he could carry around and use.

Hilltop Children's Center, Seattle, Washington

Three Dog Family Child Care, Seattle, Washington

After becoming fascinated with a book about Native Americans using canoes, these boys spent a number of weeks representing canoes of different sizes, shapes, and complexities in the block area. They incorporated symbols to represent things that were historically important in Native life. Building on this interest, the teacher supplied them with cardboard, foam board, and tape so they might try their ideas and make their canoes with a different set of tools and materials.

Burlington Little School, Seattle, Washington

Hearing these boys discussing aspects of the room arrangement, their teacher introduced the idea of map making as a way of representing spatial relations and the locations of things in the room. This generated interest in mapping floor plans, which the teacher further supplemented by introducing some commercially made floor plans. The children went on to map other things in the neighborhood.

Martin Luther King Jr. Day Home Center, Seattle, Washington

To introduce his toddlers to the idea of songbooks, one caregiver created a handmade book with pictures to represent the different songs they sing together.

Infant Toddler Center, Pasadena, California

This room has a large atlas in the block area, and the children regularly refer to it as they act out travel stories.

Burlington Little School, Burlington, Washington

Hilltop Children's Center, Seattle, Washington

Putting photos and observation stories in notebook binders gives children experience with turning to books for reference. When shown a documentation story of the representation he had made the day before, this boy immediately called it "the directions" for making the representation again.

When his caregiver took his picture, the flash caught this baby's attention, and he stared at her intently. She brought the camera up close for him to see how his image was captured on the display screen. He looked intently, smiled, and then pointed at his picture. Activities like this set the stage for children to learn that images can stand for real objects. And what better way to learn than with a concrete picture of oneself, family members, pets, or friends!

Hilltop Children's Center, Seattle, Washington

As these boys created exploding volcanoes in the block area, their teacher gave them large sheets of paper and markers to represent the volcano in another form and incorporate it into their drama. This transformed their explosive energy into a concentrated work effort.

Burlington Little School, Burlington, Washington

When she noticed that children were attracted to the sunflowers she had placed on the table, this teacher gave the children pens and paper and suggested they look closely at the flower and then draw it, so that they would still remember what it looked like after it died.

The children's drawings are kept in an accessible place, and this child decided to take one to the chalkboard and represent the same image there. Each time a child changes the medium he is working with, he faces new cognitive challenges and learns new things about what he is trying to represent.

Hilltop Children's Center, Seattle, Washington

Martin Luther King Jr. Day Home Center, Seattle, Washington

An overhead projector invites children to represent ideas in a larger scale. Here children traced their block structure as it was projected on the wall. Changing scale when re-representing ideas often reveals misunderstandings or new ideas to be explored.

Burlington Little School, Burlington, Washington

Learning to see the details in objects prepares children not only to develop skills for reading and writing, but also to represent ideas with other media. Here the teacher placed a collection of miniature pumpkins and gourds next to paints that were similar in color. The arrangement served as an invitation for the children to represent what they saw. After working with their paints, they re-represented the basket of pumpkins with pen and ink.

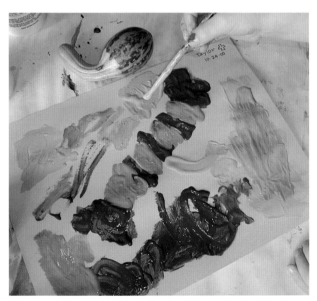

Hilltop Children's Center, Seattle, Washington

In an effort to help her preschoolers more fully explore symbolic representation, this child's teacher frequently suggests he draw something he has built, or paint something he has drawn. Clipboards and ultra-fine markers are available around the room.

Hilltop Children's Center, Seattle, Washington

After reading the Dr. Seuss book, *The Lorax,* a story about an advocate for the natural world that has no voice, the children in one preschool room leaped to their feet. They said, "We gotta make signs that tell people to take care of the earth! Signs that say 'Stop! Don't pollute! Take care of the earth!'" They hurried to the table, got paper and markers, and began to write and draw. There was a moment of uncertainty about how to proceed: "We don't know how to write words, because we're just kids." Their teacher suggested that they draw pictures that show their messages about taking care of the earth and offered to help with any words they'd like to write. "Yeah! We do know how to draw!" They took their signs out into the neighborhood and hung them on lampposts and on the front yard fence.

Hilltop Children's Center, Seattle, Washington

Babies, too, can be spurred into action by books. Rather than keeping them up high and out of reach, this caregiver places books just far enough away for them to make an effort to retrieve the one that captures their attention. She watches closely as a baby discovers the different parts of a book. She describes the parts, offering more familiarity with the concept of book covers, pages, illustrations, and words.

Kidspace Child Care Center, Seattle, Washington

Hilltop Children's Center, Seattle, Washington

The teacher in this preschool classroom invited families to send notes to their children in their lunch bags, promoting a connection to home as the children discover the value of written communications.

Martin Luther King Jr. Day Home Center, Seattle, Washington

Many parents are unsure how to become involved in the life of the classroom when they pick up their children. Here a teacher handed a parent a clipboard and suggested sitting and drawing the children's block structures. This, in turn, interested the children in drawing their block structures, helping both the parent and the child gain some initial understandings of how working with visual representations leads to emergent literacy.

To promote the idea of written communications between children and their families, the teachers in this room worked with the children to dictate letters to their parents about what they wanted parents to play with when they came to the room for an evening parent meeting. The parents arrived to find the letters and, with encouragement from the teachers, followed the children's wishes and explored the suggested materials. In turn, they wrote letters to their children to be discovered in the room the next morning. The teacher documented the parents' activities to accompany these letters.

Hilltop Children's Center, Seattle, Washington

Seeing her teacher making use of sticky notes, this child asked if she could write one with a message to her mom about what she wanted for dinner. She put the note on her mom's mailbox and then read it to her when she arrived.

Martin Luther King Jr. Day Home Center, Seattle, Washington

Inventions for Your Program...

Our profession has long advocated that programs have a print-rich environment to expose children to the value of literacy. As you expand your thinking about the world of symbolic representation and how this relates to language and literacy development, what are some new insights you have? What changes might you want to make in your environment? Consider these areas:

- Places where adults can model literacy, symbolic representation, and the visual arts
- Opportunities for decoding, translating, and reading
- Representational materials and writing tools
- A studio space
- Examples of visual artists, young and old
- Expressions of family partnerships

Once you have decided on a focus for improvements, spend some time further developing concepts discussed in this chapter that you are less familiar with. You can find some related resources in appendix A and many more in catalogs or Web listings developed by early childhood professional organizations or presses. Deepening your insights into how an environment sets the stage for children's emerging literacy and interest in the visual arts will enable you to continue to add new elements. Remember to work on your outside as well as inside environment, and your hallways and bathrooms as well as your classrooms.

Hilltop Children's Center, Seattle, Washington

Enhancing Children's Use of the Environment

7

Hilltop Children's Center, Seattle Washington

Look Inside...

Take some time to carefully study this photo and the story below and then consider the questions that follow.

A s the morning began, Ann sat on the floor in a discussion with three children, while nearby, another group was building with blocks on a wooden platform. The rest of the class was playing in other parts of the room or eating breakfast and conversing with another teacher. Ann and the children sat in a flexible area of the room furnished with a number of open-ended materials: unit blocks, logs, a basket of fabric and clips, tape measures, portable screen dividers, two stepladders, two three-foot-square platforms, and two huge cardboard tubes. The children had the idea of creating an obstacle course, and Ann suggested they gather to make a plan.

As different children came up with ideas, Ann restated them for the group's consideration. She asked some initial questions that led the children to the idea of measuring the things they wanted to include in their course. The planning then progressed, with growing excitement and some competing ideas. One child wanted to put a stepladder at each end of a cardboard tube. Someone offered the idea of covering the opening of the tube with fabric. This idea was refuted by a different child who wanted to clip the fabric as a canopy from the step stool to the tube. Ann facilitated the discussion with comments like, "Tell us your idea about how this might work," and "Could I make a different suggestion, to make sure you're safe?" She kept the group focused by continually pointing to the different objects they wanted to use as she restated the ideas they had reached agreement on. As time went along, a few more children approached the group asking if they could be involved too. "Definitely," Ann responded, "come and help us think about it." As one child struggled to explain his idea of creating an angled tunnel with two tubes, Ann suggested he get one of their reference books to explore how this might look. He brought the book back to the group and began to search through the pages for what he wanted. Ann asked, "Do you want to find it by just going through the pages or look at that list in the front of the book called the table of contents?" Later, she suggested he might get a clipboard to sketch a representation of his idea for the group.

As the obstacle course began to take shape, Ann asked the one child still working nearby on block building, "Would you like a screen around you to keep you separate from the obstacle course?" When he said yes, she assisted by putting the screen in place.

- What strikes you about the physical environment in this story?
- How would you describe the elements of the social-emotional environment that helped shape this story?
- What routines and practices might be part of how Ann structures time for these children?
- What do you think Ann's values and goals are for living and learning together in this environment?

Perhaps you have found new ideas among the examples of environments, materials, and activities in this book, and you are eager to make some changes in your physical environment. But transforming the physical environment is only part of the work to be done. Designing beautiful spaces and finding engaging materials is obviously an exciting undertaking, but there are other aspects of creating an environment that require careful attention and nurturing.

In programs like the one in the above story, the pooling of ideas and negotiating how to use the environment doesn't magically happen on its own. The teachers have created an underlying emotional climate that supports the children's use of the environment. The emotional climate reflects and fosters the values that shape their time with children. The emotional climate is intricately related to the program's daily routines, use of time, and activity structures, as well as the beliefs, expectations, and choices the adults have for the children. At the heart of the social-emotional environment are the qualities of the relationships among the people in it.

As you've studied the photos and ideas in this book, you possibly have some skepticism or doubt in your mind. You might find yourself thinking, *How many children do these teachers have in their room to be able to do these things? Don't the children break or lose things? How do they keep track of everything? What do they do about cleanup with so much available for the children to use?* These are common questions. We can assure you that the programs reflected in the photos you've seen have many of the same constraints you do. By and large, they don't have huge budgets, ideal spaces, or extra staff members. In order to understand how they have been able to make changes, it's important to examine again how teachers view children and the nature of their work. The teachers in these programs have all spent time thinking and talking about their understandings of and dreams for the work they do together. Without this careful examination and dialogue among coworkers in a program, the social-emotional environment may undermine children's ability to make productive use of the physical environment you have worked so hard to create.

Whenever young children are gathered in groups, the potential for overstimulation, competition for space and materials, and less-than-desirable behavior is great, as group energy feeds off itself and stress and anxiety rise. This is why teachers often put so much emphasis on group management and child guidance techniques. When the voices and bodies of young children become increasingly active, teachers tend to respond by restricting choices, emphasizing classroom rules, and threatening punishment. This often starts a chain reaction, and soon our view of children becomes diminished and our desire to control them escalates. But if you remember how valuable children's explorations, dramas, messy play, and conflicts are to their learning, you can make other choices that will keep your planning and responses grounded in a belief that children are capable of remarkable undertakings.

Rather than repeated reminders to pay attention and stay on task, children benefit from an environment and activities that are specifically designed to focus their attention and give them a set of steps to follow for using tools and mastering something they want to accomplish. If we want children to learn to be thinkers, rather than mere rule followers—and if we want them to conceptualize, concentrate, be intentional in their choices and uses of materials, and collaborate with others—we need an environment that specifically promotes these things.

The social-emotional environment includes how people relate to one another, how time is structured, and how the teaching and learning process unfolds. The emotional climate is shaped by what teachers choose to pay attention to and make visible and their thoughtfulness in setting up routines, choices for children, and teaching activities. Here are four areas to examine as you seek to enhance children's use of the environment.

- Time and routines
- Invitations, special interest areas, demonstrations, and modeling
- Meaningful jobs
- Teacher roles

Organizing Time and Routines

Once your room is thoughtfully arranged, it is important to plan for long periods of self-directed play. If children are to initiate their own activities, use the materials in complex ways, and have enough time to work with others, teachers mustn't chop up their time into little boxes on a schedule, or constantly direct or interrupt their activities. Children need enough time to become familiar with the environment and the ways the materials can be explored and used. They benefit from support and coaching to develop initial communication and collaboration skills. Then they will be able to make effective use of long, uninterrupted blocks of time to pursue their interests. When teachers continually redirect children's activities according to a schedule, the flow of children's intention and investigation is interrupted, and children experience disrespect for their earnest desire to demonstrate what they know or care about.

Your schedule should include stretches of uninterrupted choice times that are at least an hour long, and as the school year progresses, can extend to ninety minutes or more. During these long stretches of play or project time, close observation enables teachers to distinguish between creative exploration and random, unfocused play. When children are genuinely engaged in a pursuit, they should be respected and not made to stop and clean up before expanding their activity into another part of the room. To prevent the room from getting too messy and children from losing their focus, teachers can continually work behind the scenes to keep order and maintain the visual figure-ground relationships that will invite the children's ongoing involvement. This might sometimes include leaving one child's creation in an area as an example for another child to draw upon, a strategy that can also be used between morning and afternoon groups using the same classroom.

Ample time should be provided for cleanup at the end of the extended free choice time. Everyone can participate in cleaning up the entire room, which eliminates the cry of "I don't have to clean up, I didn't play there." When it reflects their lives and interests, children will learn that returning the room to good order can be a source of pride and productive endeavor for the next time they use the area. During cleanup teachers can demonstrate how to care for the materials, and how order and organization will alert the group to more ideas during the next play or project time. Consider using cleanup songs which also convey these values, such as the Pointer Sisters recording of "We Are Family" or the Sweet Honey in the Rock song "Oh My Goodness, Look at this Mess" from their recording *Still the Same Me*. Cleanup can be busy and noisy and take a long time. Relax and let go of the idea that cleanup should be an orderly, quick, and quiet process. You should allow ample time, have patience, and be actively involved as you work with the children on the important job of maintaining a wonderful environment.

Four Techniques to Help Children Focus and Learn to Use Materials

Children's lives today are filled with television, computer games, and toys that others have designed for them. They are continually entertained and directed in ways that trivialize their inherent quest for learning, rather than earnestly challenged to pursue a love of learning. As a result, many children who come to our early childhood programs don't have experience with self-directed play or with having their pursuits respected and enriched by the adults around them. They need guidance to recognize the possibilities for independent use of the environment. And they need assistance in discovering what their peers have to contribute to their enjoyment and learning process. Here are four techniques you can use to help children learn to focus and work with others.

DESIGNING SPECIFIC INVITATIONS AND ACTIVITIES

Once you have explored the values you want reflected in your program and have designed your physical and social-emotional environment to include respect, uninterrupted blocks of time for investigation, and opportunities for problem solving and collaboration, you can turn your attention to the details of selecting particular materials for exploration or representation. When you believe that children are curious, capable, and eager to make connections and learn, you won't rely on expensive curriculum packages or learning materials to ensure particular outcomes or test scores. Instead, you will draw on your knowledge of child development, your observations of children's play, favorite memories from your own childhood, and a creative eye as you move about the world to discover innovative materials to offer.

There is a delicate balance between offering a range of interesting materials and avoiding clutter and an over-emphasis on "stuff." Communicating the value of creating and building relationships over acquiring and consuming things involves careful thought and attention to detail. When children come upon a cluttered shelf with a pile of materials in textures and colors that have no relationship to each other, they are less likely to be able to see what is available for their use. The way materials are stored and presented sends a message to children about how the environment is valued. If they live in mess, disorder, and clutter, they will likely create more disorder, rather than using the materials thoughtfully. Your selection and combination of materials can provoke curiosity, inventions, and theory building when you take the time to intentionally and attractively arrange things as an invitation for learning. Here are some guidelines to consider.

- Arrange and store materials in attractive containers and in an inviting, orderly fashion so children can see what is available for their use.

- Highlight a collection of materials on an inviting piece of fabric, a mirror, or a tray, which emphasizes the figure/ground relationships and visually frames the activity.

- Suggest uses for materials by combining different materials.

- Display a photo near the arrangement showing how children have used this material in the past. Include a book, diagrams, or photos that suggest or spark possible uses.

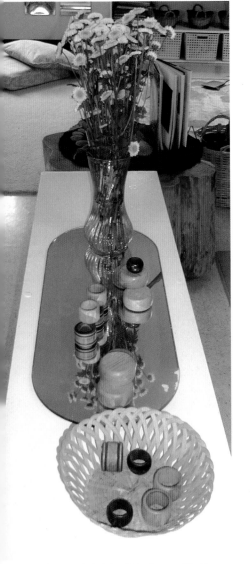

Burlington Little School, Burlington, Washington

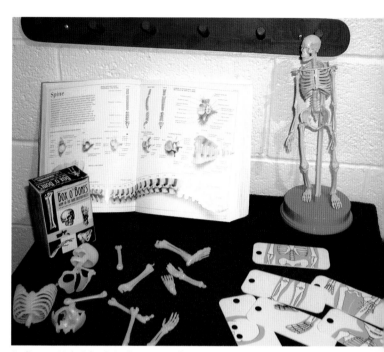

Burlington Little School, Burlington, Washington

*New City Family Center, Chicago Commons Child
Development Program (Head Start), Chicago, Illinois*

Hilltop Children's Center, Seattle, Washington

SPECIAL INTEREST AREAS

When teachers notice a recurring focus in the children's play, you can extend the possibilities by creating an area for further exploration and study. Displaying photos and examples of previous play and adding new props will keep the play going. As the children arrive each day, they will eagerly seek out ways to continue their pursuits. For example, after watching the children use straws in the water table to blow objects around, you might add new objects for exploring air. This creates the potential for a long-term study of wind or air pressure based on further observations of the children's pursuits.

Hilltop Children's Center, Seattle, Washington

Hilltop Children's Center, Seattle, Washington

DEMONSTRATIONS

Many cultural groups in the United States, as well as the Italian educators of Reggio Emilia, have provoked a reexamination of the notion that it is damaging to children's creativity to have teacher demonstrations. When done thoughtfully and with the goal of enhancing children's pursuit of their own ideas, demonstrations can help children understand the possibilities of materials and tools. College instructor Tom Drummond recommends regularly planned times for demonstrations of materials or tools. These demonstrations can be done in small or large groups and can last anywhere from five to fifteen minutes, depending on the children's interest. Throughout the year, demonstrations may be extended as the children become eager for more instruction. After a teacher demonstrates, the children are given the opportunity to explore the materials and tools for themselves without further instruction or demonstration unless requested by a child. Examples of possible demonstrations include the following:

- A variety of structures you can make with different shaped blocks
- Many ways to use a paintbrush
- How to make playdough or goop
- Different lines and curves you can cut with scissors
- Ways to examine a flower so you can draw it
- Possibilities for designing with pattern blocks
- How to work with clay and specialty clay tools
- Ways to negotiate a conflict

Once a group of children has discovered an effective process or mastered a skill, they can create demonstration charts, directions, or instruction booklets for their peers as they continue to explore materials.

MEANINGFUL JOBS

If children are to feel a part of the group and to make an investment in using and caring for the environment, then we must give them opportunities to contribute and participate in meaningful ways. Children know the difference between their world and that of adults. In addition to wanting adults to enter their world and play with them, they see adults as powerful and competent and want to be a part of that world. This is especially true when it comes to the materials and tools they see adults using. Children love to be involved with real work. They gain skills and a sense of pride, accomplishment, and ownership from making meaningful contributions to the organization, maintenance, and repair of their environment. Even toddlers want to help carry, fix, build, wash, plan, and organize things. They develop a strong identity and a sense of both independence and interdependence when they participate in activities that contribute to the classroom and program community.

Rather than trivial jobs made up by the teacher to promote self-esteem, involve children in the real work that needs to be done in your daily life together.

Organize and provision the environment so that the children can accomplish the work to be done. Children jump at the chance to use real brooms, feather dusters, lightweight vacuum cleaners, sponges, and spray cleaners as a part of a job. They feel competent and stay at a task when they use real hammers, screwdrivers, and duct tape. Strategies that will involve children in taking responsibility for housekeeping and maintenance include the following.

CLEAN-UP KITS

Let the children do the real cleaning, vacuuming, and washing. Create an area of the room with the tools the children will need. Provide child-size brooms, dust pans, and lightweight vacuum cleaners. Have an accessible storage area for cleaning equipment such as spray bottles, sponges, window cleaner, tubs, buckets, and dish towels. Make sure these are visible and well organized for the children's self-direction. Alert them to the cleaning supplies that are for adult-only use, and keep these dangerous chemicals out of their reach.

MEALTIME PREPARATION, SETUP, AND CLEANUP

Setting the table, serving food, and cleaning up are all valuable tasks. Rather than just an occasional cooking project, provide routines for the children to help with daily food preparation and cleanup. For example, children can help to plan the menu, count or weigh ingredients, follow visual recipes, or use cleanup stations to help clean up after a snack or meal.

CLASSROOM MAINTENANCE AND REPAIR WORK

Have a tool kit or cupboard organized in your classroom so children can help tape ripped books, fix broken toys or equipment, mend fabric tears, change batteries, and so forth.

Teacher Roles that Support Children's Activities

Maintaining the social-emotional environment for children's learning requires that teachers be flexible and responsive. Sometimes you are needed right in the thick of things to model and coach communication skills, the collaborative process, and problem solving. At other times your involvement might send the wrong message—that you don't value or trust what children are doing. The work of a teacher is like that of an improvisational artist, continually watching, accepting invitations, offering new possibilities, and keeping the children's ideas at center stage with attention and curiosity. Many professional resources discuss the roles teachers can play in early childhood settings—for example, *The Play's The Thing* (Jones and Reynolds 1992), *Reflecting Children's Lives* (Carter and Curtis 1996), and *Authentic Childhood* (Fraser and Gestwicki 2002). In lieu of an in-depth discussion here, consider this outline of general roles you can play to help children use and work with others in your wonderful environment.

PLAYMATE

Children benefit from having teachers model the use of materials and social skills for cooperative play. As you play with the children, focus on following their lead, observing and assessing how to support and challenge them to go deeper in their thinking with the activities and with each other.

PROP MANAGER

As described earlier, an important role for teachers during children's play is to stay alert to the need for reorganizing materials to keep the children's activities and collaborative endeavors going. This might mean offering an additional prop to support what the children are doing—either bringing it to them or suggesting they retrieve or make it. Being a prop manager might also mean that you tidy up behind the scenes, rearranging materials back into an invitation if they are in disarray or cleaning up paintbrushes, bits of playdough, and the like. The idea here is not to be policing the materials, but allowing the children to stay focused and engaged. You might also find a way to include uninvolved children as you move about attending to props.

OBSERVER AND DOCUMENTER

As the children play, you can watch closely, take notes and photographs, and sometimes videotape or make an audiotape of their activities and interactions. When this documentation is played back to the children, they get a further picture of productive ways to use the environment. They learn more about each other. They experience a way to communicate respect for someone else's work. Broadcasting or making visible what is happening creates an attentive, appreciative social-emotional environment, which, in turn, fosters healthy development of individual and group identity. Broadcasting strategies may include the following:

- Describe what you see children doing in the moment. Call the children's attention to interesting things other children are doing.

- Use the instant playback on a digital or video camera to show and talk about what the children have just done.

- Create displays with descriptive words and photos on the walls, in picture frames, and in notebooks, and place them in the areas where the children have been using the materials. Refer to these photos as sources of ideas and inspiration as the children revisit these activities.

RESEARCHER AND COLLABORATOR

You can study and discuss your observation notes and documentation data with your coworkers and the children's families to gain deeper understanding of what the children are doing, saying, and making. This will give you ideas of how you might enrich the environment, rearrange some materials, or invite the children into some further representational work. Teachers who bring curiosity, respect, and responsiveness to their work create a social-emotional environment that communicates a sense of "we," a value that children will absorb and begin to offer in return.

COACH

Early childhood teachers can often be heard reminding children to use their words, take turns, share, and "be nice to your friends." These social skills come no more automatically to children than do using the toilet, cutting with scissors, or learning to read and write. Children need patient coaching, extended time to practice, and motivational reminders of how these skills will be of use to them. Even babies benefit from this kind of environment, where confidence in their social abilities and desire to learn is communicated. Whatever age group you work with, you can create peer group experiences where children learn to listen to and "read" each other, negotiate ideas and choices, and work together to solve problems.

For instance, adapting an activity for small group experiences developed by the Tribes program, preschool teacher Ann Pelo uses the idea of "Spicy Work Group" time to help her full-day children expand their possibilities for collaboration and play with others. Ann periodically invites small groups of children who don't often play together to develop a plan for collaborative exploration of something. She discovered that children love the idea of "spicy" and come to understand that it means they might need to try a little harder to work things out with another person. Spicy work groups expand the children's social groupings and help them learn how to work things out when they have different ideas.

You can also promote collaboration by referring children to one another for ideas or help with something they are trying to accomplish. For instance, when children ask you for help, or you notice someone needs comfort or a problem solved, ask which of their peers might like to try helping. Depending on the situation, it might be helpful to suggest some ways to be helpful, or you may trust that the children have enough experience or desire to initiate their own idea. Eventually you might work with the children to develop a new kind of "jobs chart," one with the names of children who can be turned to for help with tying shoes, pouring water, mixing paint, negotiating conflicts, soothing a hurt, applying ice or a bandage, and so forth.

For many other ideas about creating an environment of inquiry and collaboration, look for the books by kindergarten and first-grade teacher Karen Gallas (all published by Teachers College Press). For example, in *Talking Their Way into Science* (1995), Gallas describes how she worked with her group to let them know the boys were dominating their science talks. She developed one strategy of telling the children who were gathered for discussion to look around for anyone who was trying to get a word in. When some boys still found it hard not to dominate the conversation, she assigned them to be "the lookers." Their job was to look around and point to people who were trying to say something, so the group would see that someone wanted to contribute. She also suggested that the children trying to get in the discussion invent a signal so the others would see them. Gallas offered the children phrases they might use to learn from one another. For instance, she might say to a child, "If you don't understand what someone has said, you could say, 'Do you mean . . .?' and try to ask a specific question." Finally, she began asking the children to acknowledge if someone's idea triggered a thought for them. She suggested that they say which child's comments led them to this thinking. This helped the children see that they could build on each other's thoughts and develop collective ideas. Rather than making rules, taking charge, and solving problems for children, Gallas's work shows that coaching children into negotiation skills, collaborative discussions, and work habits will facilitate their effective use of the environment.

Inventions for Your Program...

A combination of design elements in your physical and social-emotional environment will send a message about your values. Use the following questions to consider your own thoughts and practice, and choose an area you would like to work on in your program.

- Has your team given collective thought to the values you want your program space and routines to communicate?
- Are there features in your room that could be expanded to accommodate at least two children? For instance, a bench in front of a computer, rather than a single chair; a double easel rather than a single one; a bike with a trailer rather than just one seat; a double baby swing or a hammock?
- What demonstrations of materials or interactions would benefit the children in your program?
- What new teacher role would you like to weave into your practice?
- Do you have any new routines for collaborating or taking a new or different perspective that you want to offer to the children?
- What changes do you want to make in how you present materials that invite children's investigation and learning?

You are striving to create an environment that respects and honors children, is free from commercialization, and limits adult direction and control. You may discover that this kind of environment is new for children, and that they will need some initial guidance and routines to help them use the environment effectively. This is especially true if they are new to initiating, negotiating, collaborating, and problem solving within a group of peers.

Facing Barriers and Negotiating Change

Burlington Little School, Burlington, Washington

Look Inside...

"Children are miracles. Believing that every child is a miracle can transform the way we design for children's care. When we invite a miracle into our lives, we prepare ourselves and the environment around us. We may set out flowers or special offerings. We may cleanse ourselves, the space, or our thoughts of everything but the love inside us. We make it our job to create, with reverence and gratitude, a space that is worthy of a miracle! Action follows thought. We can choose to change. We can choose to design spaces for miracles, not minimums." Anita Rui Olds

If you saw your work in the manner Anita Olds describes as, "creating a space worthy of a miracle," how might your thinking and actions change? What strengths do you already have that you can build on? What barriers will you need to overcome?

More often than not, early childhood educators avoid bigger dreams for our programs because we feel we don't have adequate resources. Barriers to reaching our vision seem daunting and insurmountable. The overall goal of most programs is to stay in compliance with minimum licensing standards. If they are professionally active and feeling ambitious, program directors will sometimes undergo the self-study process for voluntary accreditation with the Academy of the National Association for the Education of Young Children (NAEYC). But if we think of children as miracles, deserving of dreams, rights, and respect far beyond minimums, early childhood professionals must take up the challenge of overcoming barriers and pushing beyond the limited attention and resources allotted to our field.

When we first think of barriers, we focus on things such as lack of financial resources, staff turnover, building limitations, and the lack of public will for policies and legislation to make children an economic priority. These are indeed serious challenges, ones requiring tenacity and ongoing activism. But before we can approach these hurdles, we have to face down the barriers inside ourselves—the attitudes, limited thinking, and isolation that hold us back. Looking over the inspiring photographs in this book and considering the examples of strategies for transforming an environment, it's possible that your head is filled with responses such as, *"There's no way I can do that. They won't let me,"* or *"That would never fly with my director (or my licenser, or Head Start federal review monitor,"* or *"There's no way we'd have the money for that."* Perhaps you've had real experiences where roadblocks were put in front of something you were trying to do, or maybe you've heard stories of others failing to get approval or money for an exciting idea for their program.

But think again. Surely you have a memory of a time you overcame a barrier—something to remind you that this can be done.

Internal Barriers

The most difficult barriers are not the external ones, but the ones inside yourself. These can be a fear or a hesitancy to take a risk. You may feel as though making changes would put yourself, children, or your program in jeopardy. Fears are important to examine and face in the light of day. Our first priority is always to keep children and programs safe. But so often, imagined fears take on lives of their own and get entangled with a person's timidity, struggle for self-acceptance, or a sense of powerlessness.

Other internal barriers can be an unconscious belief that you don't deserve something better, that you shouldn't make waves, or that you should stop dreaming and be willing to settle for what you have now. You might find yourself subject to "either/or" thinking, which can create an inability to get past that first "no" and negotiate with differing perspectives. Sometimes a lack of knowledge, information, skill, or experience can be a barrier. All of these roadblocks can be dismantled with determination, perseverance, new understandings, and a healthy sense of humor.

Think of a time when you successfully overcame a barrier inside yourself like this. Dig through your memory and come up with a specific experience of pushing past some hesitation, a limited self-concept, fear, or prevailing attitude. What was this situation? What made it possible for you to get over the barrier that was in your way? Have you had an experience where facing down your inner roadblocks has led to overcoming a barrier outside yourself, such as a policy, regulation, or lack of immediate resources? Have you ever heard someone else tell a story like this? If you were to draw some lessons from this experience, what would they be?

Consider stories of well-known people who have overcome tremendous barriers to reach their dreams. For instance, Wilma Rudolph contracted polio as a young child, which paralyzed her left leg, and doctors told her she would never again walk. With determination and support from her family, she first mastered walking with the use of a brace. Eventually she discarded the brace and went on to become the first American woman to earn three gold medals in one Olympics. Furthermore, the parade to honor Wilma in her Tennessee hometown was the first celebration there to include blacks and whites socializing together. As we read her biography, we learn the elements that allowed her to hurdle the physical limitations before her—strong concentration, determination to never give up, a supportive family, and an enduring faith.

There are also inspiring stories of early childhood teachers who have overcome significant barriers as they stretched their respective programs to meet a bigger vision. For instance, Ann Pelo and Sarah Felstiner, two teachers at Hilltop Children's Center in Seattle, Washington, first taught alone in separate rooms at Hilltop and felt tremendously discouraged by the isolation. On separate trips, each of them visited the schools of Reggio Emilia, and they returned to Seattle eager to transform their work. Their program is located on the second floor of a church building, and the possibilities for transforming the space were limited. They longed to knock down some walls between the classrooms, but were told the church would never allow such a thing. So, instead, they knocked down the walls in their minds, schemed to reconfigure the use of their two rooms, and approached their director with all the details mapped out.

They transformed the smaller of their two rooms into a studio space, put their combined children, furniture, and materials in the larger room, and began to team teach. Ann and Sarah have inspired other teachers in their program to make similar changes, and now their work has been featured in several videos (*Children at the Center, Setting Sail, Thinking Big,* and *Building Bridges between Teachers and Families,* filmed with a teacher across town, Deadru Hilliard, who was also transforming her attitude and space). People from around the country come to visit their program, and they draw inspiration for how to transform less than desirable spaces into beautiful environments.

There are four major internal barriers that must be overcome in the early childhood field if we are to successfully tackle the external barriers. These internal barriers often overlap and create a sense of futility and hopelessness in us.

- A fear of taking risks and thinking outside the box
- A scarcity mentality
- Isolation
- A feeling of powerlessness

Because our profession is full of regulations needed to hold providers accountable to keeping children healthy and safe, and because the United States is a litigious culture, it's easy to adopt the attitude of "I wouldn't dare," or "They won't let me." While extremely important risk management issues must be addressed, this shouldn't put our thinking in a box or make us think that reaching for a bigger dream is a risk too big to take. In *The Visionary Director* (Carter and Curtis 1998), we offer a number of strategies for beginning to nourish a vision for your program, acknowledging the tendency of early childhood providers to keep our expectations low to avoid deep disappointment. A scarcity mentality plagues our field, and because early childhood people are so used to living with hand-me-down spaces and materials, we begin to think we don't deserve or can't get access to something better.

The work and stress within one child care program is usually so overwhelming that directors and teachers have a hard time getting out of their own buildings and connecting with others in the profession. The job can be very isolating with little time or energy left over to explore what others are doing to improve their quality, overcome barriers, or keep their dreams moving forward. When people are tired, they don't remember that getting out and exercising their bodies and brains will energize them, not further exhaust them. Likewise, when people are short on time they forget that making time to explore other ideas will expand their sense of possibilities.

While it's true that there are barriers outside of ourselves, perhaps the biggest barrier is a person's internal feeling of powerlessness. It's easy to forget that you do have a tremendous amount of power in your program, starting with your attitudes, the organizational climate you create, the physical space you design, and the materials you present to children. You have control over these things. They communicate your values and intentions and in turn, shape how you feel and behave while in the space.

"There's so much more we have control over than we give ourselves credit for. I decided to stop making excuses and start taking action. The first thing I did was to transform our large utility and storage room into a beautiful staff lounge. This was tricky because we never have enough storage, but the room was always such a dumping ground that no one ever kept clean. I decided to stop being the nag about it and just try something new. I went to several of those storage stores for ideas and also did a search for articles and Web sites with bright ideas for small spaces. For a little over a thousand dollars I put in a much more organized and effective storage system, enclosing the washer and dryer and water heater; I set up a work counter with a computer station, got a love seat, two lamps, end tables, and a stuffed chair. There weren't any windows in the room so I had to settle for painting a mural of a window with a nature scene outside and setting up some grow lights for plants. This was one of the best investments I ever made. It not only gave respect and assistance to the staff, but gave them a new 'can-do' attitude. All sorts of other positive changes began to grow out of this first step. When you do something bold in behalf of yourself and your staff, it has a snowball effect for the change process you want."

Janet Read, child care director, Kidspace, Seattle, Washington

External Barriers

When asked what external barriers get in their way to creating the kind of environments promoted in this book, providers typically identify one or more of these four concerns.

- Shared space
- Licensing regulations
- Staff turnover
- Lack of resources

You may not have a facility where you have to share rooms with another group, such as a church, synagogue, mosque, or community center, but you no doubt face the other three barriers providers usually identify. While each early childhood setting has its own unique issues, we all face some common aspects in programming for young children. Getting together with other providers is a terrific way to discover these shared issues, hear strategies that have been successful, and develop a collective voice to advocate for change. Through the National Association for the Education of Young Children (NAEYC), its local affiliates and publications, journals such as *Child Care Information Exchange,* and an ever growing list of chat rooms and e-mail discussion groups on the Internet, you can discover groups that have formed around a common context or set of circumstances such as campus-based or church-housed programs, military programs, programs located in Jewish community centers, or out-of-school programs. Becoming part of an organization or Internet group will bring you out of isolation and give you a support system for concerns particular to your situation.

NEGOTIATING SHARED SPACE

Providers who work in space shared with another group find it a tremendous challenge to continually set up and take down the environment they have created. Sometimes early childhood or out-of-school programs use social halls or gymnasiums that must often be cleared out for special events regularly hosted by the group that owns the building. Many programs just assume that this would not be feasible, so they don't try to create an attractive and inviting environment for children, but operate instead out of toy boxes and locked cupboards. When renting space in a building that is used for Sunday school on the weekends, a secular program may have religious materials throughout the room, creating a dilemma.

Some part-day programs, such as Head Start, nursery school, or pre-K classes, have double sessions with two different groups using the space in one day. When this involves a different teaching staff for each session, a system must be developed for how to organize the room to accommodate the approach and materials each might have. Whatever the particulars, programs that have successfully negotiated a way to share space with another group or teaching team all say that building friendly relationships, shared understandings, and mutual respect is the key to making it work. Here are examples of some of the things they say.

"You have to start by assuming you will have to compromise, but that doesn't mean lowering your standards or giving up your dreams. Approaching each other without resentment or blame is key. I've found that sometimes just beginning to beautify the space in simple ways, for instance with plants, lamps, and attractive rugs, creates an appealing environment for the church group as well as my child care kids. When I wanted to make bigger changes, like putting acoustic tiles and fabric banners on the ceiling to absorb the sound and soften the feel of this cavernous social hall, I went to the church with some drawings and catalog pictures and explained how I thought this would be good for both of our programs in this space. A combination of these approaches has worked well for us. Sometimes it has even resulted in sharing the cost of improving the space."

Mari Kennedy, after-school program coordinator, Big Kids Program, Mesa, Arizona

"Every Friday we need the preschool to take down and put in storage all their materials so that we can use the space for our church functions. On numerous occasions they tried to persuade us to allow them to leave some things up, but our deacons were never willing to agree to that. The preschool purchased a number of rolling cabinets and installed hooks and Velcro strips in various places on the walls to facilitate their setup and breakdown process. Still, each Friday and Monday it took them about an hour and a half to go through this routine. Our attitude was that this was just their problem to deal with. At some point we realized that if we wanted them to stay and we stood to benefit from the rental income, then we needed to meet them half way. We devised a plan where we paid our custodian to come in to do that ninety-minute breakdown each Friday and the preschool paid for the ninety-minute setup person on Monday mornings."

Cassandra Wilkins, church pastor, Little Angels Preschool, Tacoma, Washington

"For years I grumbled about the things I couldn't do because of the double sessions in our Head Start where a different set of kids and teaching team used my room each morning. We'd meet at the beginning of every school year to set up the room together according to the Creative Curriculum and it stayed that way all year long. But then I'd get different ideas when I'd go to conferences or see pictures of other classrooms and it would start to irritate me that I couldn't make any changes because the morning teachers wanted to keep things the same. I kept thinking that maybe someday we'd get some different morning teachers, but that just didn't happen. Finally my coordinator came up with the idea that all morning and afternoon teachers in the same room should go together to attend the same workshop sessions at the conference. She also made it a policy that every three months we would evaluate how the space was working in our room, taking turns as to who had the final say over what we would change. We did this for a couple of years and then gradually began to be more open to each other's ideas and desired changes. I think the real turning point came when I got to get rid of the busy, bright-colored carpet in the room, add a couch and some lamps to make the place more homey. This just mellowed out the behaviors in the morning as well as afternoon group and before long, one of the morning teachers came in with a big plant she wanted to find a place for."

Reba Kaushansky, Head Start teacher, EOC Head Start, Portland, Oregon

CREATING A PARTNERSHIP WITH LICENSERS AND MONITORS

There are many compelling reasons to be a strong advocate for highly regulated early childhood programs, not the least of which is educating and holding providers accountable for the health, safety, and education of young children. In nearly every state in the United States, at least one monitoring agency oversees group care of children, usually including some combination of fire, health, safety, and staffing regulations. In some states the requirements are bare minimums, while in others they are more fully developed. In addition to government regulatory bodies, professional and agency contractual agreements try to define higher quality standards for programs to adhere to, such as the Early Childhood Rating Scale, the self-study process of NAEYC accreditation, the Center on the Childcare Workforce model work standards, Montessori and High/Scope certification, and so forth. Each of these has its set of best practices, and there is considerable overlap in the content of the standards and assessment processes they use. The overall intent of regulating, licensing, certifying, and monitoring programs is to keep providers and teachers aware and accountable for managing risk and the well-being of children. .

Over the last couple of decades, agencies responsible for assessing and overseeing programs for young children have continually expanded and reorganized, and most have begun to require their monitoring specialists to have an early childhood education background. This is an important development, particularly at the state licensing level, because monitors with specific early childhood programming experience usually understand not only the intent of the regulations, but also what well-meaning providers are trying accomplish when they seem to step outside the letter of the law. Hopefully there will be fewer stories of rigid interpretations that misdirect the intent of regulations, for instance thinking that a child-centered classroom means there is no adult furniture, or that keeping things at children's eye level disallows a model of a solar system to be hung from the ceiling.

Most regulations are written as general guidelines for providers to follow to ensure that children will not be subjected to any undue risk and that activities will be age appropriate. Because many of these guidelines are subject to interpretation, some regulators, with the goal of being consistent and fair, have taken it upon themselves to create a specific definition of how the requirements should be translated into practice. Some want to eliminate any trace of risk potential and thus require strict adherence to their understanding of the regulations. Others focus on the intent of a regulation and are open to different ways that it might look. In either case, it is a regulator's job to hold us accountable for the lives of children in our care, and we should be grateful that they take their work seriously. As one fire department inspector said, "If you have had to carry a child in flames out of a burning building, you will never be lax about fire safety regulations."

Providers, teachers, directors, regulators, and licensers are all trying to do what they think is best for children. Conflicts arise when they have different priorities and different interpretations about what this means. Rather than assuming antagonistic positions, forming a partnership between regulators and programs on behalf of children's welfare should be the goal. A partnership, by necessity, always involves mutual respect, good communication skills, negotiation, and a willingness to compromise or develop alternatives together. As programs try to implement the ideas in this book, typical issues around which this partnership must come into play include the following:

- Hanging fabric or any potentially flammable materials in the room
- Ceramic or breakable glass objects
- Free-standing tall furnishings, or cabinets
- Recyclable loose parts
- Ladders, lofts, swings, or multi-tiered structures
- Free-standing or tabletop lamps
- Plants, animals, rocks, logs, sticks, or water
- Ropes, nets, hammocks, tires, hoses, or adult tools
- Holes, hiding places, or jumping places

Important issues arise around the use of these materials, and in each case, the negotiation process must take into account such things as the following:

- Overall compliance with health, safety, and risk management issues
- Philosophy and goals of the program
- Size, age, and competence of the group of children
- Adult-child ratio
- Staff training and proximity and skill of adult supervision
- Space configuration and established protections
- Safety audit, sanitation, and maintenance systems
- Provisions made for geographic susceptibility to hazardous acts of nature such as earthquakes, tornados, and floods

Professional safety auditors who work with the National Playground Safety Institute and follow the guidelines of the Consumer Product Safety Commission rate the seriousness of hazards from a priority number-one hazard, which can cause death or permanent disability, to a priority number-three hazard, which may cause minor injury such as scrapes or splinters. Drawing on this model, when their licensing office took over responsibility for outdoor play space inspections, a group of licensers in Washington State led the effort to educate other licensers and develop resources for this new work. They put together a guidebook, a training for licensers, and a notebook for orientations that includes the Accident Pyramid (see facing page). Marjorie Johnson, a licenser in Washington State, says,

"It is critical that we look at programs situationally and get the bigger picture of what they are trying to do. We need to help them get knowledge, skills, and abilities. Let's look at the intent of the regulation. What's good for children's development? We need to get away from a strictly prescriptive, one-size-fits-all approach and gather a body of knowledge. How could this look different than what I imagined and still meet children's needs? I once worked with a licenser that made a program take out their rosebushes because they had thorns. Now, I'd kind of like kids to discover that thorns will poke you and you need to be careful around them. We have to notice where the true risks are and focus on preventing life-changing accidents, while allowing childhood to flourish in all its many dimensions."

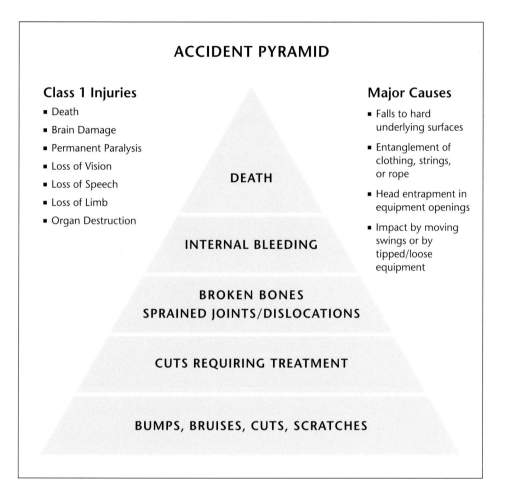

Using the Accident Pyramid they developed for their trainings, Johnson explains it as follows.

- Most injuries are at the bottom of the pyramid.

- Fewer injuries are at the top of the pyramid (Class 1 injuries).

- We cannot prevent all bumps, bruises, minor cuts, and scratches. They are part of the experience of childhood.

- We *must* prevent Class 1 injuries by identifying the major causes and eliminating the hazards that tend to cause them.

In speaking with other licensers and program directors around the country, we have heard some wonderful examples of the attitudes, relationships, and thoughtful negotiations that create meaningful partnerships between providers, regulators, and monitors.

"My licenser recognizes that I have gone through a long, tedious process to make these changes. She sees that I work with a vision and not a catalog as I create the environment I want for the children. For instance, seeing that I had a chicken in the backyard for the children to interact with and feed didn't alarm her. She saw that we are always on guard when the children are out there and we aren't lax about washing hands when they come in. I now feel good about my work. I can look people in the eye and say with pride, 'I'm an excellent family provider.' My licenser thinks so, too, because she brings new licensers to visit our program."

Vic McMurray, Bridges Family Child Care, Madison, Wisconsin

"Negotiating is what it's all about. Providers need to know that. They can negotiate with us. They really can. Providers come up with options all the time. I always tell them, if you have a good idea, I'm going to put it in my little album to show everybody at the new provider orientation meetings. Two examples come to mind. One provider found a way to create the required barrier between the diaper changing stations. She put up a piece of sheet metal and then got hook magnets and hung clipboards with the diaper changing charts on them. That was real neat. Another provider wanted to put infants on the second floor and was faced with what to do about the requirement for an evacuation crib for babies. She did some research on the Internet and found an 'evacuation apron' made in Quebec and approved throughout Canada. The apron has pockets for putting the babies in and easily carrying them in an emergency. That was such a good solution and she came up with it. Of course we would accept that and I'm going to recommend it to others."

Marge Sorlie, state public health specialist, Seattle, Washington

"My experience shows that if you can get the people with clout into your center, it goes a long way toward solving the dilemmas that come up. Even before our official licensing visit we contacted our licenser to give her some information about the Reggio approach and how we were approaching curriculum. We said, 'Why don't you just come in and visit apart from your monitoring role?' She spent a lot of time reading our documentation panels and began to understand that our approach to planning involved responding and logging down what was happening, rather than using the required weeklong planning approach. We used webs to hypothesize about the meaning of what was happening and used items from it to add to our daily plan. This plan actually became a log, because we often changed things as the day evolved. We included in our plan a box that says, 'changes to make to the environment.' Her response was, 'If there are new ways you want to do it and I can see that rich things are happening for the children, then that's enough for me.'

That taught me that if we want to do something we believe is good for kids, then we should challenge a regulation and see what happens. These people are human beings. As long as you have a rationale that you can show them, you can change these old scripts. Government agencies can be very intimidating, but no one is going to take away your license if they see a good program. If enough of us question some of these things, they are likely to go back and reexamine the regulations. They need to evolve, just like we do."

Susan Stacey, program director, New Hampshire
Technical Institute, Concord, New Hampshire

"If a provider calls me for a consultation or a request for a waiver, when I am in agreement with their intent and am convinced that there is no logical reason to prevent an approval, I will seek the support of people above me to address their concern. Where there is no precedent, for instance, in the case of a program that wanted a ferret for a pet, we consulted with an expert in the field, and negotiated from there. From the vet we learned that ferrets are able to be vaccinated so we could approve this with that stipulation. I've negotiated fixing loft railings that are too far apart with sheets of Plexiglas. We were able to flexibly interpret the intent of bolting cabinets to the wall by allowing a hook and eye security system to allow more flexibility for rearranging the furniture. As people are trying to make things more aesthetically pleasing, they may inadvertently raise a fire safety hazard. It's interesting to notice my first reaction and then with further thought, to be willing to work with them to meet their goals. These issues require thought and money. I try to encourage people to spend money at the outset on quality materials and prevention strategies rather than replacing things all the time. Quality lasts. It doesn't create a good impression for the children, parents, or licensers if things are always in need of repair.

Kathy O'Neill, child care licensing specialist, Concord, New Hampshire

"There are things I take far more seriously now than I did as a director, for instance, having visual, not just auditory access to the infant napping area. When I sign my name to that piece of paper as a licenser, it means I'm responsible for saying that this is a good and safe program for children. There have now been five SIDS deaths in child care programs in our state. This hadn't happened when I was a director. Given my caseload and the time I have available to observe in a program, I find I have lowered my expectations, especially compared with doing a day long NAEYC accreditation validation visit. I mainly have to focus on health and safety issues. When I see something alarming, like the way ropes have been hung like nooses on a playground, I have to tell myself to keep breathing, just to bring my tension down. This breathing helps me remember I need to observe carefully to see how skilled and effective the teachers are at supervising the children, and then to negotiate with, rather than jump on them.

I'd really like to see rails on risers and protective padding around any thin edges. But I also want to educate providers to know they can negotiate with me. Lamps make me nervous, but I'll accept them if they are held down with sturdy Velcro."

Jean Kasota, child care licenser, Seattle, Washington

"Every director in the room told me I was crazy to want a little stream or pond on my play yard. What I've discovered is that because nobody has done these things, it's assumed this won't be allowed. But no one has attempted to ask or offer their own way to address the intent of the regulations. I ask my licenser, 'How can I do these things? Please talk to your supervisor.'"

Dee Jammal, child care director, Smart Start, Dallas, Texas

"I have goals. I am not a person to back down when I face barriers. For one thing, I don't wait for a problem before getting to know my licenser. I invite her to stop by, let her know what we are trying to do, and call her when we've made changes. She can see that the children are thriving, the parents are happy—and so is the staff. We are all learning and growing. I get my paperwork in like she wants. We have averted any real problem with licensing and we are doing some rather unconventional things inspired by the Reggio approach."

Julie Garrett, Head Start center director, Karen D. Love Neighborhood House Association Head Start, San Diego, California

"For many years the fire marshals in our state oversaw these inspections with no early care and education background. All they knew was health and safety. It reminded me of the proverb which says something like, 'If all you have is a hammer, then everything looks like a nail.' I think most problems with licensers arise when we don't know how to ask about what we are seeing. When something concerns me, I've trained myself to say, 'Tell me what goes on here,' and to observe very carefully. Maybe it doesn't meet the licensing regulation, but maybe it's not as scary as I thought. I'm looking for providers to tell me, 'Here's what we do. Here's why. And here's how we keep kids safe.' That's the first step in getting a waiver approved when you need one.

Charlotte Jahn, child care licenser, Seattle, Washington

TAKING ON STAFF TURNOVER

There is no easy solution to the problem of staff turnover, a well-substantiated undermining factor for achieving and maintaining quality in early childhood programs. The problem is a complex systemic one, and now a number of players are working on state initiatives aimed at financing the education and training attached to incremental salary enhancements. The jury is still out on the promise of these efforts, and many teachers and providers are calling for a guarantee of livable wages before additional training is required. A combination of sustained community organizing, teacher and provider presence at decision-making tables, and a host of public awareness and policy efforts will be necessary to adequately resolve the child care staffing crisis. In the meantime, programs can address their own working conditions, organizational climate, and budget allocations to motivate staff to become activists and to stay long enough to see these systemic changes through.

Ultimately a workplace with an engaging, nurturing environment; beauty and attention to detail; good communication systems and democratic management principles; and opportunities to design, invent, and collaborate makes people want to stay. Along with this book, there are several valuable resources to assist you in making your program an attractive, viable place to work. The following books all have concrete strategies to try.

Bellm, Dan, and Peggy Haack. 2002. *Working for quality child care.* Washington, D.C.: Center for the Child Care Workforce.

Bloom, Paula Jorde. 1997. *A great place to work: Improving conditions for staff in young children's programs.* Washington, D.C.: NAEYC.

———. 1998. *Creating better child care jobs: Model work standards for teaching staff in center-based child care.* Washington, D.C.: Center for the Child Care Workforce.

———. 2000. *Circle of influence: Implementing shared decision making and participative management.* Lake Forest, Ill.: New Horizons.

Carter, Margie, and Deb Curtis. 1998. *The visionary director.* St Paul: Redleaf Press.

Whitebook, Marcy, and Dan Bellm. 1999. *Taking on turnover: An action guide for child care center teachers and directors.* Washington, D.C.: Center for the Child Care Workforce.

TRANSFORMING YOUR THINKING ABOUT RESOURCES

It is hard to imagine an early childhood staff that feels it has enough resources. Whether they operate for profit or not, whether large or small, nearly all programs feel they can't get closer to their dreams without additional resources. Programs always need more money, more time, and more staff. They also need more vision. And as programs grow and refine their visions, they will uncover resources they never imagined.

Sometimes there are resources right under our noses that we haven't tapped: ideas to inspire us, models to visit, expertise from other fields, stories and relationships to nourish our souls. While it's true we need more money, money alone isn't what's holding us back. We need to transform our thinking about resources and expand the field of vision we work with.

"Most programs wait until they have money before they work on clarifying their vision. I've learned how important it is to write down our vision and continually refine our goals and action plans. I don't want to settle for small results. We are going for more than what seems possible at any given moment."

Karen Haigh, Head Start director, Chicago Commons
Child Development Program, Chicago, Illinois

Creating a rich environment in your program takes a significant amount of time if you don't have a lot of money and resources. It takes time to collect low-cost, interesting equipment and materials, and time and patience to stumble across a great bargain, treasure, or find! It also takes a change in your mindset about what materials and equipment would enrich your program. Move away from an institutional school mentality and think about the kind of place you want to spend your days. This means shopping in places other than early childhood catalogs or children's stores.

Thrift shops, garage sales, creative recyclable and surplus stores, and estate sales can be great sources of materials and equipment. Make sure you choose things that are clean and in good repair. Just because something is secondhand doesn't mean it needs to be junky. Here's a list of places and what to look for as you scrounge through the piles and aisles.

THRIFT STORES, GARAGE SALES, AND DOLLAR STORES

- Baskets ranging anywhere from ten cents on up. Don't pay any more than two or three dollars unless the basket is really special. You can get brand new baskets at discount stores for the same price. Look for flat baskets where materials can be seen easily in your displays. Removing handles from baskets makes them a lot easier to use. On the other hand, if they are for infants and toddlers, leave the handles on.

- Wooden trays, bowls, dishes, and cutting boards. Again, look for flat bowls and trays to display items. Many of these wooden pieces have dividers and make great containers for displaying a variety of items or for children to sort objects.

- Glass jars, vases, and bottles. These can be used for storing things so you can see them. They can also be used for presenting paint, glue, and water for water coloring. You might additionally like to use some interesting glass objects, bowls, or plates for work on the light table.

- Furniture for making a cozy environment. You can sometimes find great deals on end tables, shelves, and couches in good condition in these places. Estate sales are usually the best source of quality used furniture.

- Stuffed animals and props for animal play. Kittens, puppies, rabbits, dog bowls and leashes are all abundant from thrift stores and garage sales at bargain prices.

- Hardware and appliances. Visit the hardware and appliance section of your stores looking for things that move—nuts and bolts, pulleys, and other treasures—to make into contraptions for children's exploration.

- Various treasures. You never know when you'll find a special item that you and the children will fall in love with. Napkin rings, bags of artificial flowers, mirrors, knickknacks, interesting game pieces, scarves, fabric pieces, and jewelry are often available. You can even find an occasional quality toy at a very discounted price.

- Plastic containers. These are abundant sources for plastic containers, sorting trays, colored dishes for the light table, and other interesting containers and implements for sensory exploration and transformation.

- Frames and book stands. Dollar stores are a great source for wooden and Plexiglas frames for displaying photos, documentation, and art. They also carry an array of stands for holding up books.

- Plastic toys. Be wary of most of the junky plastic toys that are available in discount places. But you can find snakes, lizards, kitties, puppies, and bugs for a dollar a bag that can be used in many of your invitations. Collections of glow-in-the-dark letters, numbers, and shapes work well on the overhead projector.

- Knickknacks. Seek out small items made of glass such as swans, tropical fish, and tiny shoes that can be displayed as a part of a tabletop treasure. If you spend less than a dollar, you don't have to worry if they accidentally break. You can find a bag of 100 marbles for a dollar too!

GARDEN STORES, PLANT NURSERIES, AND CRAFT STORES

Garden stores are great sources for natural materials, and many will offer discounts to nonprofit programs. When you shop carefully, you can also make use of some craft materials that portray the natural world well.

- Natural materials. Look for dried flowers, pods, and gourds, as well as living plants and flowers (see appendix A for recommended nontoxic plants for early childhood programs). You can also find stones, shells, rocks, beach glass, and glass stones, along with larger boulders, bricks, and stepping stones. Of course, you may live in a place where these can be gathered from the natural world, but take care to protect the ongoing supply from Mother Nature.

- Artificial flowers and figurines. Craft stores, in particular, carry a variety of artificial flowers, fruits, vegetables, and leaves that are lovely for play and display (avoid the plastic ones and choose those made of feathers and fabric). You can also find sweet representations of birds, bugs, butterflies, and bird's nests made from natural materials and feathers.

- Sand, rocks, and pebbles. You can buy bags of different colored washed sand (black, sparkly white, and volcanic red are all wonderful in a sensory table or tray). Bags of rocks and pebbles can be used in sensory trays too.

MUSEUM GIFT SHOPS

The gift shops in children's and adult museums, science centers, art galleries, botanical gardens, and national parks require you to spend a bit more money for what you find, but they often have unusual and fabulous items to include in your invitations for children.

- Light and color objects. Try to find prisms, holograms, color cubes, kaleidoscopes, special lights, and other things for exploring light and color.

- Nature posters, postcards, books, games, and figurines or models. Seek out print resources with beautiful illustrations, photographs, stories, and representations of the natural world.

- Math and physics games and experiments. You can find an array of interesting objects for investigating physics and motion and other natural phenomena including such things as perpetual motion machines, mobiles, magnets, displays of the solar system, and so on.

- Art prints, postcards, and books. You might also find quality art materials and unusual gift items like sculptures and glass figures. Look for these in art supply stores as well.

SPECIALTY SHOPS AND ETHNIC STORES

Stores which specialize in imported items from other countries offer a range of materials, so spend time looking for quality, but inexpensive, items.

- Asian dishware and utensils. These bowls and plates are usually small and come in a variety of shapes and beautiful patterns. You can choose glass or plastic and use these wonderful containers for all kinds of things from the sensory table to the drama corner.

- Fabric, purses, and musical instruments. You can find beautiful fabric from every part of the world to soften and beautify your program. You can also find unique musical instruments like shakers, drums, and bells.

- Animal and people figures. These are often made of wood, leather, or fabric with whimsical and realistic features.

FAMILY AND COMMUNITY CONNECTIONS

Some of the best sources of wonderful materials, furnishings, and other items come from the families in your program or members of your community. You can make specific requests for donations from these people or explain the general idea of what you are looking for. Many families are willing to donate good quality furniture or carpets that they may be replacing in their homes. In fact, they may have a garage or basement full of useful items that they would love to donate. Community organizations have volunteers who are often willing to donate money or labor to a project you would like to complete. Asking people to be involved in your program, with specific requests, gives them a way to be a part of a community of people that supports children and childhood.

Rather than only viewing limited resources as a barrier, consider this as an opportunity to go on a treasure hunt. Base your choices on things that will extend what you see children already doing or discussing, or things that will give them a new perspective on something familiar. Remember that the value is in promoting a focus on relationships, rather than consuming and amassing "stuff."

A Journey of Hope

If we think of children as miracles in our lives, they will inspire us to hurdle barriers and transform things that aren't worthy of a miracle. Miracles tend to beget miracles, so once you take this approach to designing your program for living and learning with children, be prepared for some new joy and satisfaction in your work. And, goodness knows, your attitude and transformative work is likely to have a ripple effect, changing the tide in how early care and education is viewed and practiced. Thank you for joining us in this commitment to a journey of hope for our children and ourselves.

Appendix A: Resources

With the constantly expanding Internet resources at your fingertips, it would be impossible to list a definitive selection of resources. Instead, we have chosen sites we are familiar with and can recommend that will expand your understanding of the ideas in this book. See p. 214.

Books—Background Reading for Concepts

Alexander, Christopher, Sara Ishikawa, and Murray Silverstein. 1977. *A pattern language*. New York: Oxford University Press.

Carter, Margie, and Deb Curtis. 1998. *The visionary director: A handbook for dreaming, organizing, and improvising in your center*. St Paul: Redleaf Press.

Day, Christopher. 1990. *Places of the soul: Architecture and environmental design as a healing art*. San Francisco and London: The Aquarian Press.

Gallagher, W. 1993. *The power of place: How our surroundings shape our thoughts, emotions, and actions*. New York: Simon and Schuster.

Gandini, Lella, and Cathy Topal. 1999. *Beautiful stuff: Learning with found materials*. Worcester, Mass.: Davis Press.

Hart, Roger. 1978. *Children's experience of place*. New York: Irvington Press.

Hirst, K. H. 2000. *Recipes and ideas: Storage*. San Francisco: Chronicle Books.

Kritchevsky, Sybil, and Elizabeth Prescott. 1969. *Planning environments for young children: Physical space*. Washington, D.C.: NAEYC.

Nabhan, Gary, and Stephen Trimble. 1994. *Geography of childhood: Why children need wild places*. New York: Beacon Press.

Parent, Marc. 2001. *Believing it all*. New York: Little, Brown and Company.

Rivkin, Mary S. 1995. *The great outdoors: Restoring children's right to play outside*. Washington, D.C.: NAEYC.

Storey, S. 2000. *Recipes and ideas: Lighting*. San Francisco: Chronicle Books.

Wagner, Tony. 2001. *Making the grade*. New York: Routledge.

Books—Early Childhood and Out-of-School Environments and Programming

Bellm, Dan, and Peggy Haack. 2002. *Working for quality child care*. Washington, D.C.: Center for the Child Care Workforce.

Bloom, Paula Jorde. 1988. *A great place to work: Improving conditions for staff in young children's programs*. Washington, D.C.: NAEYC.

Cadwell, Louise Boyd. 1997. *Bringing Reggio home*. New York: Teachers College Press.

———. 2002. *Bringing learning to life*. New York: Teachers College Press.

Center for the Child Care Workforce. 1998. *Creating better child care jobs: Model work standards for teaching staff in center-based child care*. Washington, D.C.: Center for the Child Care Workforce.

Curtis, Deb, and Margie Carter. 1996. *Reflecting children's lives: A handbook for planning child centered curriculum*. St Paul: Redleaf Press.

Fraser, Sue, and Carol Gestwicki. 2002. *Authentic childhood: Exploring Reggio Emilia in the classroom*. Albany, N.Y.: Delmar

Fu, Victoria, Andrew Stremmel, and Lynn Hill, eds. 2002. *Teaching and learning: Collaborative exploration of the Reggio Emilia approach*. Upper Saddle River, N.J.: Merrill-Prentice Hall.

Gandini, Lella. 2002. The story and foundations of the Reggio Emilia approach. In *Teaching and learning: Collaborative explorations of the Reggio Emilia approach*. Edited by Victoria Fu, Andrew J. Stremmel, and Lynn T. Hill. Upper Saddle River, N.J.: Merrill Prentice Hall.

Gardner, Howard. 1983. *Frames of mind: The theory of multiple intelligences*. New York: Basic Books.

Greenman, Jim. 1988. *Caring places, learning spaces*. Redmond, Wash.: Exchange Press.

Greenman, Jim, and Ann Stonehouse. 1996. *Prime times: A handbook for excellence in infant and toddler programs*. St Paul: Redleaf Press.

Hendrick, Joanne, ed. 1997. *First steps toward teaching the Reggio way*. Upper Saddle River, N.J.: Prentice Hall, Inc.

Illinois Facilities Fund. 2000. *Great spaces, fresh places: How to improve environments for school-age programs*. Chicago: Illinois Facilities Fund.

Isbell, Rebecca, and Betty Exelby. 2001. *Early learning environments that work*. Beltsville, Md.: Gryphon House.

Jones, Elizabeth, and Gretchen Reynolds. 1992. *The play's the thing: Teachers' roles in children's play*. New York: Teachers College Press.

Kolbe, Ursula. 2001. *Rapunzel's supermarket*. Sydney: Peppinot Press.

Lally, Ron. 1994. *Together in care: Meeting the intimacy needs of infants and toddlers in groups*. Sacramento, Calif.: Program for Infant/Toddler Caregivers (PITC) of WestED Center for Child and Family Studies and the California Department of Education Child Development Division.

Prendiz, Marcella. n.d. *It's all in the presentation: The value of children's art displayed in the classroom.* Seattle: Harvest Resources, forthcoming.

Seefeld, Carol. 2002. *Creating rooms of wonder.* Beltsville, Md.: Gryphon House.

Topal, Cathy Weisman, and Lella Gandini. 1999. *Beautiful stuff: Learning with found materials.* Worcester, Mass.: Davis Publications, Inc.

Williams, Leslie, and Yvonne De Gaetano. 1985. *Alerta: A multicultural, bilingual approach to teaching young children.* Boston: Addison Wesley.

Books and Articles—Safety, Building, and Landscaping Designs

Berry, Pauline. 2001. *Playgrounds that work: Creating outdoor play environments for children birth to eight years.* Baulkham Hills (Sydney) NSW, Australia: Pademelon Press.

Ceppi, Giulio, and Michele Zini, eds. 1998. *Children, spaces, relations: Metaproject for an environment for young children.* Reggio Emilia: Reggio Children and the Commune di Reggio Emilia.

Consumer Product Safety Commissions. 1997. *A handbook for public playground safety.* Washington, D.C.: U.S. Government Printing Office.

Dannenmaier, Molly. 1998. *A child's garden.* New York: Simon and Schuster.

Keeler, Rusty. 2000. *Soundscape recipe book.* Ithaca, N.Y.: Planet Earth Playscapes.

Miller, Norma, ed. 1995. *The healthy school handbook.* Washington, D.C.: NEA Professional Library.

Moore, Robin. 1993. *Plants for play: A plant selection guide for children's outdoor environments.* Berkeley, Calif.: MIG Communications.

Moore, Robin, Susan Goltsman, and Daniel Iacofano, eds. 1992 *Play for all guidelines: Planning, designing, and management of outdoor play settings for all children.* Berkeley, Calif.: MIG Communications.

Olds, Anita. 2000. *Child care design guide.* New York: McGraw-Hill.

Senda, Mitsuru. 1992. *Design of children's play environments.* New York: McGraw-Hill.

Smart Start. 2002. *Children's outdoor environments: A guide to play and learning.* Raleigh, N.C.: National Smart Start Technical Assistance Center.

Stine, Sharon. 1996. *Landscapes for learning: Creating outdoor environments for children and youth.* New York: John Wiley & Sons.

Sustainable Buildings Industry Council. 2002. *High performance school buildings resource and strategy guide.* Washington, D.C.: Sustainable Buildings Industry Council.

Weinstein, C., and T. G. David. 1987. *Spaces for children: The built environment and child development.* New York: Plenum Press.

———. 2002. *Making a place for children: Child care facility planning manual for Washington State.* Olympia, Wash.: State of Washington.

ARTICLES

Beginnings Workshop. 2001. Environments. *Child Care Information Exchange* (November).

Beginnings Workshop. 2002. Environments with families in mind. *Child Care Information Exchange* (September).

Caesar, Betsy. 1999. Playground safety for the twenty-first century. *Child Care Information Exchange* (September).

Forman, George. 1996. Negotiating with art media to deepen learning. *Child Care Information Exchange* (March).

Heschong Mahone Group. 1999. Daylighting in schools: An investigation into the relationship between daylighting and human performance. Available at www.h-m-g.com.

Hurwitz, S. 1999. The adventure outside your classroom door. *Child Care Information Exchange* 127 (May).

Moore, Gary. 1997. Houses and their resource-rich activity pockets. *Child Care Information Exchange* 113 (January/February).

———. 1997. The common core of a child care center. *Child Care Information Exchange* 114 (March/April).

Moore, Robin. 1989. The early childhood outdoors: A literature review related to the design of child care environments. *Children's Environments Quarterly* 6 (Winter).

Sussman, Carl. 1998. Out of the basement: Discovering the value of child care facilities. *Young Children* 53, no. 1 (January).

Wardle, Francis. 1987. Getting back to the basics of children's play. *Child Care Information Exchange* 57.

———. 1990. Are we taking play out of playgrounds? *Day Care and Early Education* 18, no. 1.

———. 2000. Supporting constructive play in the wild. *Child Care Information Exchange* (May/June).

Videos

Carter, Margie. 1997. *Children at the center: Reflective teachers at work*. Seattle: Harvest Resources. Available at www.ecetrainers.com.

Carter, Margie, Sarah Felstiner, and Ann Pelo. 1998. *Thinking big: Extending emergent curriculum projects*. Seattle: Harvest Resources. Available at www.ecetrainers.com.

Curtis, Deb, and Margie Carter. 1997. *Setting sail: An emergent curriculum project*. Seattle: Harvest Resource. Available at www.ecetrainers.com.

Greenman, Jim, and Muriel Wong Lundgren. 1998. *Great places for childhoods*. Redmond, Wash.: Child Care Information Exchange.

National Institute of Out of School Time (NIOST). 2000. *A place of their own: Designing quality spaces for out-of-school time*. Boston: NIOST. Available at www.wellesley.edu.

Program for Infant/Toddler Caregivers (PITC). 1997. *In our hands*. Sacramento: PITC of WestED Center for Child and Family Studies and the California Department of Education Child Development Division. Available at www.pitc.org.

———. 1997. *Ten keys to culturally sensitive child care*. Sacramento, Calif.: PITC of WestED Center for Child and Family Studies and the California Department of Education Child Development Division. Available at www.pitc.org.

Wolpert, Ellen for the Committee for Boston Public Housing. 1999. *Start seeing diversity*. St. Paul: Redleaf Press.

Web Sites

Children's Environment Research Group, web.gc.cuny.edu
The Children's Environment Research Group of City University of New York conducts research projects and archives back issues of the journal they published from 1984–1995. They also host a Listserv discussion group about children's environments.

ERIC Digest, ericeece.org and ericece.org/reggio.html
An online source for the ERIC Clearinghouse on Elementary and Early Childhood Education at the University of Illinois. Maintains an extensive list of articles, book reviews, and archived Listserv discussions.

Harvest Resources, www.ecetrainers.com
The Web site for Deb Curtis and Margie Carter's consulting services, Harvest Resources, offers early childhood education training tips, books, and videos.

The International Association for the Child's Right to Play, www.ipausa.org
The International Association for the Child's Right to Play offers valuable resources and information on their international work.

International Secretariat for Child Friendly Cities, www.childfriendlycities.org
A listing of international resources focused on the rights of children.

KaBOOM! www.kaboom.org
A site with extensive resources to assist communities in coming together to develop playgrounds.

National Recreation and Park Association, www.nrpa.org
The National Recreation and Park Association Web site provides up-to-date information on playground safety.

Natural Learning Initiative, www.naturalearning.org
The Natural Learning Initiative is a research and extension program of the University of North Carolina that offers resources and project ideas for outdoor play areas.

New Village Schools, www.newvillageschools.org
This Web site was started by Harvard educator Tony Wagner. Here Wagner details his New Village Schools, which emphasize the need to reinvent rather than reform schools.

Planet Earth Playscapes, www.planetearthplayscapes.com
The official Web site of Rusty Keeler and Planet Earth Playscapes offers an amazing array of resources and links for planning early childhood environments, with a special focus on environmentally friendly materials and sensory-rich natural playgrounds. You will find a great focus on building environments with families and communities.

Roots for Change, www.rootsforchange.net
The official Web site for the Early Childhood Equity Alliance provides a comprehensive network for people interested in discussions and resources about culturally relevant anti-bias programming and in undoing racism work.

Spaces for Children, www.spacesforchildren.net
This Web site features quality facility design. Former early childhood educator Louis Torelli shares very useful ideas for setting up developmentally appropriate spaces for young children.

United States Consumer Product Safety Commission, www.cpsc.gov
Consumer product information including an up-to-date list of recalled products.

Selected Commercial Vendors

Back to Basics Toys, One Memory Lane, Ridgely, MD 21685-8783, 800-356-5360;
www.amazon.com

Challenge and Fun, P. O. Box 222, Ashland, MA 01721, 888-384-6200;
www.challengeandfun.com
Challenge and Fun is a distributor of unique children's furniture and toys, especially
from European vendors such as Eibe.

Community Playthings, P. O. Box 901, Route 213, Rifton, NY 12471; 800-777-4244;
www.communityplaythings.com
Serving as a long-time advocate for giving children a childhood, this vendor is one
of the most reliable producers of wood furniture and unit blocks for children's programs. In recent years they worked closely with Anita Olds.

Dr. Drew's Toys, Inc., P. O. Box 1003, Boston, MA 02205; 617-282-2812;
dr-drew@iu.net
Dr. Drew's Toys carries wonderful sets of small natural wood blocks and planks.

Evacu-5, 106, Michener, Cap-de-la-Madeline, Qc., Canada G8T 1V8; 819-376-0209
This is a great resource for specially designed evacuation aprons (see chapter 8).

Hearthsong, P. O. Box 1050, Madison, VA; 22727-1050; 800-325-2502;
www.hearthsong.com

IKEA stores. Various locations.
IKEA is a wonderful source of attractive furniture, rugs, storage units, and children's
toys. To find the one nearest you visit www.ikea.com.

Insect Lore, P. O. Box 1535, Shafter, CA 93263; 800-LIVE BUG; www.insectlore.com
Insect Lore offers a variety of science and nature materials, including live insect kits
for hatching, worm kits, science equipment, incubators, puzzles, books, and posters.

Learning Materials Workshop, 274 North Winooski Ave, Burlington, VT 05401;
800-693-7164; www.learningmaterialswork.com
Here you can find an impressive selection of Froebel-inspired wooden toys and learning materials kits. Some materials draw on influences from Reggio as well.

Mindware, 121 Fifth Avenue NW, New Brighton, MN 55112; 800-999-0398;
www.mindwareonline.com
Carrying an interesting line of what they call "brainy toys" for kids of all ages, this
organization has a nice selection of wooden toys and games—even their plastic
games are more interesting than most; they have an especially suitable selection for
school-age programs.

The Nesting Company, 5417 Valley View Road, Rancho Palos Verdes, CA 90275;
888-663-3377; TNCPM@aol.com
Drawing influence from Reggio Emilia, this vendor has a lovely line of nest-like cribs
and open-ended modular wooden furniture.

The Olive Press, 5727 Dunmore Drive, West Bloomfield, MI 48322-1613;
800-797-5005; theolivepress@yahoo.com
In addition to a variety of lovely books, this press distributes the latest titles from
Reggio Children.

Ten Thousand Villages, P. O. Box 500, Akron, PA 17501-0500; 717-859-8100;
www.tenthousandvillages.com
This company distribute artisans' handicrafts from developing countries around the
world, including textiles, musical instruments, dolls, and pottery.

Torelli/Durrett, 4010 Calhoun Avenue, Chattanooga, TN 37407; 877-867-3171; www.spacesforchildren.net
This design group has a beautiful line of carpeted risers, lofts, ladders, tunnels, and wooden furniture for infant through preschool programs.

Uncle Goose Toys, 407 Richmond NW, Grand Rapids, MI 49504; 888-774-2046; www.unclegoose.com
Uncle Goose Toys distributes a nice selection of wooden puzzles and Froebel-inspired toys. Also has links to the Froebel network.

Sources for Loose Parts and Creative Recyclables (courtesy of Walter Drew)

Association for Resource Conservation
9 Bittersweet Court
Center Port, NY 11721
Tel: 516-355-0334
www.craftmaterialsresource.com

Classroom Materials Exchange
1821 Chelsea Street
Elmont, NY 11003
Tel: 516-355-0334

Columbia School Recycle Center
3120 St. Louis Avenue
St. Louis, MO 63106
Tel: 314-652-1659

Community Resource Recycle
 Center/NCECP
38 Montvale Avenue, Suite 330
Stoneham, MA 02180
Tel: 781-279-4658; e-mail:
ncecp@shore.net

Crayons to Computers
1250 Tennessee Avenue
Cincinnati, OH 45229
Tel: 513-482-7095; Fax: 513-643-4228
www.crayons2computers.net

The Creation Station
19511 64th Ave. W.
Lynnwood, WA 98026
Tel: 425-775-7959

Creative Educational Surplus
9801 James Circle, Suite C
Bloomington, MN 55431
Tel: 612-884-6427

Creative Re-Use/North Bay
P. O. Box 1802
Santa Rosa, CA 95402
Tel: 707-546-3340

Creative Zone
Pell District School Board
5650 Hurontario Street
Mississaugua, ON L5R 1C6, Canada
Tel: 905-890-1010; Fax 909-890-0660

Discovery Learning and Development
 Training Center
P. O. Box FH 14484
Nassau, Bahamas
Tel: 242-324-6661; Fax 242-324-0257

Donation Depot
New Hampshire College
2500 North River Road
Manchester, NH 03106
Tel: 603-644-3120
www.snhu.edu

East Bay Depot for Creative Reuse
6713 San Pablo Avenue
Oakland, CA 94608
Tel: 510-655-6628; Fax: 510-655-6536;
e-mail: eastbaydepot@hotmail.com

Extras for Creative Learning
P. O. Box 365475
Hyde Park, MA 02136
Tel: 617-635-8284; Fax: 617-635-6382;
e-mail: rfeldman@x4cl.org
www.extrasforcreativelearning.org

Florida Reusable Resources Network/
 Institute for Self Active Education
P. O. Box 511001
Melbourne Beach, FL 32951
Tel: 321-984-1018; Fax: 321-984-9090;
e-mail: dr-drew@iu.net
Listserv:
FloridaReuseNet@yahoogroups.com;
www.FloridaReuseNet.org

Gift for Teaching
Foundation of Orange County
 Public Schools
2814 Corrine Drive
Orlando, FL 32805
Tel: 407-897-3612; Fax: 407-897-3613;
e-mail: glandwirth@aol.com

Hudson Valley Materials Exchange
207 Milton Turnpike
Milton, NY 12547
Tel: 845-567-1445

Imagination Station, FCGB
47 Upson St.
Bristol, CT 06010
Tel: 860-583-1679; e-mail: darlene.hurtado@snet.net
www.familycenters.org

Kids in Need Center
Broward Education Foundation
600 SE Third Avenue
Ft. Lauderdale, FL 33301
Tel: 954-765-6237; Fax: 954-767-8576;
e-mail: BEFBurns@aol.com

Materials for the Arts
3400 Old State Road 37 South
Bloomington, IN 47401
Tel: 812-349-2876; Fax: 812-349-2872

Materials for the Arts
410 West 16th Street
New York, NY 10010
Tel: 718-719-3001

Ocean Bank Center for Educational
  Materials
900 NE 125th Street, Suite 10
North Miami, FL 33161
Tel: 305-892-5099; Fax: 305-892-5096

Ohio Reusable Resources Network
1651 Otter Court
Grove City, OH 42123
Tel: 614-871-4276; Fax: 614-871-9002;
e-mail: drogers@1waynet.net

Re:Art and More
900 Williams Avenue, Suite B
Columbus, OH 43123
Tel: 314-297-8561; Fax 614-297-8562

Recycle Shop of the Boston Children's
Museum
300 Congress Street
Boston, MA 02210
Tel: 617-426-6500, ext. 210;
Fax: 617-426-1944
www.bostonkids.org

Recycle Materials Center
Indian Springs Market Place
4601 State Avenue
Kansas City, KS 66102
Tel: 913-287-8888; Fax: 913-287-8332
www.kidmuzm.org

Recycling Program
Pasco County School District
7301 Land O' Lakes Boulevard
Land O' Lakes, FL 34639
Tel: 813-794-2752; Fax: 813-794-2133;
e-mail: mmiller@pasco.K12.fl.us

Recycling for Rhode Island Education
P. O. Box 6264
Providence, RI 02940
Tel: 401-781-1521; Fax: 401-781-2163;
e-mail: rrieorg@fortress.com
www.rrie.org

ReDO (Reuse Development Organization)
P. O. Box 441363
Indianapolis, IN 46244
Tel: 317-631-5395; Fax: 317-631-5396;
e-mail: info@redo.org
www.redo.org

Resource Depot
P. O. Box 30295
Palm Beach Gardens, FL 33420
Tel: 561-882-0090; Fax: 561-882-0091;
e-mail: watkinsgray@aol.com

Resource Place
975 North Beltline Highway
Mobile, AL 36618
Tel: 251-473-1748; Fax: 334-473-1313;
e-mail: mrsldc@aol.com

ReStore
186 River Street
Montpelier, VT 05602
Tel: 802-229-1930

Reusable Resource Activity Center
3300 N. Pace Boulevard
Pensacola, FL 32505
Tel: 850-595-5900; Fax: 850-595-5972;
e-mail: debra_pursley@hotmail.com

Reusable Resource Adventure Center
P. O. Box 360507
Melbourne, FL 32936
Tel: 321-729-0100;
e-mail: faul2247@Bellsouth.net

Reusable Resources Association
P. O. Box 511001
Melbourne Beach, FL 32951
Tel: 321-984-1018; Fax: 321-984-9090;
e-mail: dr-drew@iu.net
www.rra5.tripod.com
Listserv:
ReusableResourcesAssn@yahoogroups.com

Reusable Resource Center
Alachua County Office of Waste
  Alternatives
P. O. Box 1188
Gainesville, FL 32602-1188
Tel: 352-374-5245; Fax: 352-337-6244;
e-mail: sblythe@co.alachua.fl.us

Reusable Resources Recovery Center
P. O. Box 973
Vero Beach, FL 32961
Tel: 561-770-4607; Fax: 561-978-0432;
e-mail: carolynKIRB@aol.com

Ritenour Early Childhood Center
  Lending Library and Recycle Center
9330 Stanberry
St. Louis, MO 63134
Tel: 314-493-6245

Ruth's Reusable Resources
272 Hwy U.S. 1
Scarborough, ME 04074
Tel: 207-883-8407;
e-mail: doniebe@yahoo.com

Scrap Box
581 State Circle
Ann Arbor, MI 48108
Tel: 734-994-0012
comnet.org/scrapbox

Scrap Exchange
1058 West Club Boulevard
Durham, NC 27701
Tel: 919-688-6960

Scrounge Center for Reusable Art Parts
2000 McKinnon Avenue, Building 428
San Francisco, CA 94124
Tel: 415-647-1746; Fax: 415-647-1744

Share Center
P. O. Box 800
Auburn, Maine 04212-0800
Tel: 207-795-0972; Fax: 207-784-2969;
e-mail: sharecenter@auburnschl.edu
www.auburnschl.edu/sharecenter

St. Louis Teachers Recycle Center
1305 Havenhurst
Manchester, MO 63011
Tel: 636-227-7095;
e-mail: sltrc@juno.com
www.sltrc.com

Teacher Supply Depot
Duval County Public Schools
1701 Prudential Drive, Room 614
Jacksonville, FL 32207
Tel: 904-381-7480; Fax: 904-390-2654;
e-mail:buckleyK@ix.netcom.com

Teacher Supply Depot
Seminole County PTA Council
400 E. Lake Mary Boulevard
Sanford, FL 32773
Tel: 407-320-0310; Fax: 407-320-0286;
e-mail: judywiant@msn.com

Teacher Universe
Fischler Graduate School of Education
  and Human Services
1750 NE 167th Street
North Miami, FL 33162-3017
Tel: 954-262-8728; Fax: 954-262-3883;
e-mail: wkaryn@nova.edu

Treasure Trove Depot
Putnam County School Board/KPB
528 NCR 315
Interlocken, FL 32148
Tel: 386-684-1512;
e-mail: barber_j3@firn.edu

University of Missouri St. Louis Educa-
  tional Materials and Resource Center
Ward E. Barnes Library
8001 Natural Bridge Road B23
St. Louis, MO 63121
Tel: 314-516-6826

Wemagination Center
Family Development Institute
University of New Mexico
Albuquerque, NM 87131
Tel: 505-268-8580; Fax 505-277-6782;
e-mail: wedonate@unm.edu

Worcester Public Schools Recycle Center
211 Providence Street
Worcester, MA 01607-1199
Tel: 508-799-3629; Fax: 508-799-8237

Recommended Plants for Outdoor Play Areas

This list was compiled from a variety of resources. Many other options can be found on the Web or in gardening and landscaping books. Be sure to check which are best suited for your climate zone.

FRUIT-BEARING PLANTS

Grapes

Blueberries

Strawberries

Raspberries

HERBS

Mint

Lavender

Rosemary

Sage

Golden marjoram

Thyme

Parsley

Cilantro

Oregano

GROUNDCOVERS

Sedum

Hens and Chicks

Violets

Sweet woodruff

Forget-me-nots

Creeping thyme

PERENNIALS

Clematis

Alliums

True geranium

Columbine

False Solomon's seal

Western bleeding heart

Aster

Artichoke

Ferns

Ornamental grasses

TREES AND SHRUBS

Heavenly bamboo (nandina)

Dwarf bamboo

Paper birch

Mountain ash

Shore pine

Vine maple

Red osier dogwood

Japanese maple

Chinese witch hazel

Butterfly bush

Pussy willow

Mock orange

Hydrangea

Appendix B:
Tools for Assessing Your Environment

Preschool Assessment

Put yourself in the shoes of the three- to six-year-old children who spend their days in your space. Use the statements below (all from a child's point of view), to assess your space for child-friendliness. Write the number of each statement in all of the places on your floor plan where you are confident the statement is true.

1. I can see who I am and what I like to do here and at home.

2. There are comfortable places where my tired mommy or daddy, grandma, or auntie can sit and talk with me or my teacher.

3. The natural world can be found here (such as objects from nature, animals, living specimens).

4. There is something sparkly, shadowy, or wondrous and magical here.

5. My teacher leaves a special object out here every day so I can keep trying to figure out more about its properties and how it works.

6. There are materials here that I can use to make representations from what I understand or imagine.

7. I can feel powerful and be physically active here.

8. I can learn to see things from different perspectives here, literally and through assuming roles in dramatic play.

9. I see my name written, or I get to regularly write my name here.

10. I get to know my teacher here—what she likes, how she spends her time away from school, and which people and things are special to her.

Assessing for Family Friendly Environments

Draw a floor plan of your current facility. Rate it for family-friendly components according to the following elements and letter codes.

Put an **L**
in all of the places where families and children
can see their interests and **lives** reflected.

Put a **D**
in all of the places where families can see
what their children have been **doing** in the program.

Put an **S**
in all of the places where children and families
can learn more about the **staff** and their lives.

Put an **N**
in all of the places where children and families
can learn about what is happening in their
neighborhood and larger community.

Put a **C**
in all of the places where the children and
adults can sit **comfortably** together.

Put an **A**
in all of the places where family members
can stop and talk with the program **administrator(s).**

Assessing Your Environment for Infants and Toddlers

Draw a floor plan of your room and write these letter codes in all the places where these elements are present.

Put an **I** in all the places that children's
identity, family life, and culture are reflected and nourished.

Put an **H** in all the places where parents can feel
at **home,** relaxed, and respected in the room.

Put an **R** in all the places where **relationships** can be nourished
with special time, sharing, and enjoyment between adults and children.

Put an **SD** in all the places where there are **sensory
discoveries** and experiences for the children (such as different
textures, light pools, color, shadows, smells, sounds).

Put an **LM** in all the places where **large-muscle** activity is encouraged
(climbing, crawling, pushing, pulling, sliding, bouncing, hiding,
throwing, going up/down, up/over, in/out, and so on).

Put an **SM** in all the places where **small-muscle** skills can be
developed (grasping, banging, poking, stacking, shaking, squeezing,
patting, pouring, fitting together, taking apart, and so on).

Put a **C** in all the places that are soft and **cozy** and where
a child can get away from the group to rest or watch.

Put a **P** in all the places where the children can feel
powerful, independent, important, and competent.

Put an **A** in all the places where **adults** can relax,
enjoy, and share their lives with the children.

Put an **S** where there are **systems** for communication
and record keeping among the adults.

Assessing Your
Work Environment for Staff

Draw a quick floor plan of your building, and code it by filling in numerals for the following elements.

Put a **1** where it is clear a new staff person is being welcomed into the program.

Put a **2** where there is evidence of who the staff members are and what they do in the rest of their lives (their passions and values).

Put a **3** where one can learn the history of the program and its people.

Put a **4** where the staff can easily store their personal belongings.

Put a **5** where the staff has easy access to technology: a phone; a computer with e-mail and with technical training and support available.

Put a **6** where adults are nurtured by beauty and a relationship to the natural world (fresh air, natural light, plants, shells and so on).

Put a **7** where there is a staff work space with accessible, well-organized resources.

Put an **8** where there is a comfortable place to meet with families.

Put a **9** where staff can learn what is happening with coworkers' and children's activities taking place in other rooms.

Put a **10** where there is evidence that staff members are engaged in professional development.

Put an **11** where there is a place for staff, away from children, to relax, put their feet up, and have some quiet time to think over how the day is going.

Put a **12** where there are places for staff to have uninterrupted discussions with each other.

Put a **13** where there is evidence of accomplishments by the staff.

Put a **14** where you can see ongoing efforts to improve wages, benefits, and working conditions.

Also from Margie Carter and Deb Curtis

The Art of Awareness: How Observation Can Transform Your Teaching
By Deb Curtis and Margie Carter. Do more than watch children—*be* with children. Covering different aspects of children's lives and how to observe them, as well as tips for gathering and preparing documentation, *The Art of Awareness* is an inspiring look at how to see the children in your care—and how to see what they see.

The Visionary Director: A Handbook for Dreaming, Organizing, & Improvising in Your Center
By Margie Carter and Deb Curtis. Hear the voices of directors who have used their vision of child care to change their communities for the better. *The Visionary Director* will inspire directors to shape their own vision beyond day-to-day terms and have "bigger dreams for the role their programs can play in reshaping the communities where they reside."

Reflecting Children's Lives: A Handbook for Planning Child-Centered Curriculum
By Deb Curtis and Margie Carter. Keep children and childhood at the center of your curriculum and rethink ideas about scheduling, observation, play, materials, space, and emergent themes with these original approaches.

Training Teachers: A Harvest of Theory and Practice
By Margie Carter and Deb Curtis. Help teachers experience constructing their own knowledge and respecting their own learning styles so they can help children do the same. Some of the best ideas in teaching and learning are put into action with these innovative training tools.

Spreading the News: Sharing the Stories of Early Childhood Programs
By Margie Carter and Deb Curtis. Share the value of high-quality early childhood care and education with parents, other teachers, community member, and legislators using the ideas in *Spreading the News*.

Children at the Center: Reflective Teachers at Work (Video)
By Margie Carter. Follow teachers in two programs as they redesign their classrooms and evaluate their roles for a child-centered curriculum. This video explores exciting approaches to setup, scheduling, and curriculum planning.

Setting Sail: An Emergent Curriculum Project (Video)
By Deb Curtis and Margie Carter. See how a child's interest in a song about the *Titanic* grows into an exciting classroom project. This video examines how teachers foster artistic expression, scientific knowledge, language development, and social skills through this project.

Thinking Big: Extending Emergent Curriculum Projects (Video)
By Margie Carter, Sarah Felstiner & Ann Pelo. See how teachers discover emergent curriculum themes in children's play and extend them into in-depth project work.

Call toll-free 800-423-8309
www.redleafpress.org